Work or Welfare?

Mildred Rein

The Praeger Special Studies program—
utilizing the most modern and efficient book
production techniques and a selective
worldwide distribution network—makes
available to the academic, government, and
business communities significant, timely
research in U.S. and international economic, social, and political development.

Work or Welfare?
Factors in the Choice
for AFDC Mothers

PRAEGER SPECIAL STUDIES IN U.S. ECONOMIC, SOCIAL, AND POLITICAL ISSUES

Praeger Publishers   New York   Washington   London

Library of Congress Cataloging in Publication Data

Rein, Mildred.
    Work or welfare?

    (Praeger special studies in U. S. economic, social,
and political issues)
    Includes bibliographical references.
    1. Public welfare—United States.   2. Welfare
recipients—United States.   3. Child welfare—United
States.   I. Title.
HV91.R44   362.8'2   74-4458
ISBN 0-275-28869-2

PRAEGER PUBLISHERS
111 Fourth Avenue, New York, N.Y. 10003, U.S.A.
5, Cromwell Place, London SW7 2JL, England

Published in the United States of America in 1974
by Praeger Publishers, Inc.

In the Memory of my Father

ACKNOWLEDGMENTS

Some parts of this book were originally working papers that I wrote while employed as a Research Associate at the Social Welfare Regional Research Institute at Boston College. It grew out of my work at that institute. I would like to thank Martin D. Lowenthal, its director, for allowing me the time to enable me to write the book.

I would also like to thank my husband, Martin Rein, for his help in constructive criticism throughout the entire writing process.

CONTENTS

	Page
ACKNOWLEDGMENTS	vii
LIST OF TABLES	x
INTRODUCTION	xi

Chapter

1 ANTECEDENTS OF WORK AND WELFARE 1

    Mothers' Pensions 1
    Social Security 4
    The 1962 Amendments 10
    Notes 17

2 PATTERNS OF WORK AND WELFARE 20

    A Theory of Work and Welfare 21
    The Welfare Pattern 22
    The Work Pattern 26
    Implications 29
    Notes 30

3 DETERMINANTS OF THE WORK-WELFARE CHOICE 33

    Labor-Force Determinants 34
        Work History 34
        Education and Skill 36
    Monetary Determinants 40
        Welfare Benefits 40
        Income Disregards 44
    Cultural Determinants 50
        The Male-Female Conflict 51
        The Culture Around and Above: Welfare 54
        The Meaning of Income 56
    Conclusions 58
    Notes 59

Chapter   Page

4   WORK INCENTIVES: "THIRTY AND ONE-THIRD"   64

        The National Data   65
        Empirical Studies   67
        Tax Rates   73
        Conclusions   79
        Notes   81

5   WORK REQUIREMENTS: WIN   84

        Selectivity   86
        Differentiation   90
        Sanctions   93
        Conclusions   96
        Notes   98

6   WELFARE REFORM: FROM WORK INCENTIVES TO
     WORK REQUIREMENTS   101

        The Family Assistance Plan   103
            Provisions   103
            Work Requirements   104
            Work Incentives   106
        H.R.1   107
            Work Requirements   108
            Work Incentives   109
        The Long Plan   110
            Provisions   110
            Work Incentives   111
            Work Requirements   113
        The Talmadge Amendment   114
        Conclusions   117
        Notes   121

INDEX   123

ABOUT THE AUTHOR   127

LIST OF TABLES

Table   Page

1   Percentage of AFDC Mothers Who Work, by
        Education, 1967   36

2   Comparison of Working AFDC Mothers in Two
        Regions   39

3   Comparison of AFDC Families with Nonassistance
        Income and Income from Mother's Employment,
        for the United States and New York City   44

4   Employment and Average Earnings of Michigan
        AFDC Recipients, July 1969-December 1971   71

5   Linear Regression Analysis (Least Squares)
        Benefit Levels and Incentives as Predictors
        of Earnings, Total Work, Full-Time Work,
        and Part-Time Work, 1971   78

6   First Order Correlations of Benefit Levels
        and Incentives with Earnings, Total Work,
        Full-Time Work, and Part-Time Work, 1971   78

7   Changes in Full-Time Work, Part-Time Work,
        Total Work, and Earnings 1967 and 1971,
        by Low-Incentive and High-Incentive States   80

In one form or another, society has always been willing to maintain those who cannot maintain themselves. But when a group that is being assisted becomes too large and its support too costly, attempts are made to distinguish those in the group who can maintain themselves from those who cannot-- to separate out the nondeserving from the deserving. To single out employables is thus the essential strategy for containing the size of the assistance group under such circumstances.

The decision regarding who is employable and who is not is less a technical problem than an ideological persuasion. Its outcome depends upon such factors as the acceptability of the reason for assistance and the availability and advisability of employment: the needs of the labor market. These conditions, of course, change with changing times and climates so that the definition of an employable person changes with them.

Between changes or at times of mixed formulations, this definition may also be mixed or ambivalent. The case of mothers in the Aid to Families with Dependent Children (AFDC) program reflects such ambivalence. While it is true that the AFDC caseload is expanding at a phenomenal rate and its cost growing accordingly, such factors as a belief in individual freedom of choice, the support of minority group rights, and a concern for the psychological effects of mothering on children have tended to mitigate against a clear-cut advocacy of the employment of mothers. On the other hand, two recent phenomena have emerged that tend to favor such employment. Mothers in the nonassistance population have entered the labor force in large numbers; and it has recently been found that AFDC mothers, too, have had a great deal of work experience. Chapter 2, "Patterns of Work and Welfare," documents the close association between work and welfare in the lives of these women.

As a result of the ambivalence about work, AFDC mothers are now being given a _choice_ as to whether to work, to be supported by welfare, or to combine both. The mother, divested of male support, must choose work or welfare to maintain herself and her children. This choice depends upon many considerations: on the availability of work, her qualifications for work, the level of wages, the nuisance value of work, her concept of mothering, the cultural supports for work, the availability of welfare, the level of welfare benefits, the nuisance value of welfare, and the cultural supports for welfare. Chapter 3, "Determinants of the Work-Welfare Choice," examines the impact of some of these factors on the choice.

Since it is the thesis of this book that welfare policy is the most important of these determinants, the way policy has evolved in regard to work is traced in assistance programs from Mothers' Pensions to welfare reform. Each period will reflect the degree of societal ambivalence about work for these aided mothers. When the idea of choice is most tolerated, there is a tendency to use services and incentives as inducement strategies, while efforts to constrict the work-welfare choice entail requirements and eligibility restraints.

Chapter 1, "Antecedents of Work and Welfare," deals first with the state Mothers' Pension programs that started in 1911 and continued until the passage of the Social Security Act in 1935. They represent the outcome of the struggle between the private social agencies that had dispensed aid to fatherless children before and the advocates of state pensions for these children. Public relief was the victor, but in practice the pension philosophy, which would have permitted mothers to stay home to care for their children, became subverted into a variant of private charitable relief. The fear was that public sponsorship would ensure assistance as a right, thus encouraging huge numbers of recipients. Work was used as a containment strategy in an effort to rehabilitate the mothers through "constructive supervision."

Aid to Dependent Children (ADC) also was legislated in 1935 as a provision to enable mothers of deprived children to stay at home. The southern states, however, were loath to permit their "employable" female Negro field workers to cease work. They instituted work requirements and established low benefits and thus both compelled and encouraged ADC mothers to work. By the 1960s the ADC client body had changed: widowhood declined as a reason for assistance while broken marriages and illegitimacy increased. The size of the assistance group also drastically increased. The 1962 amendments were the first major national effort to contain the caseload through services for rehabilitation toward the goal of self-support.

By 1967 work had become the panacea for the still-growing AFDC caseload.* Both federal work incentives and

---

*The name of the program was changed in 1962 from Aid to Dependent Children to Aid to Families with Dependent Children.

federal work requirements were legislated at this time. Chapter 4, "Work Incentives: 'Thirty and One-Third,'" evaluates the efficacy of this disregard of earned income in terms of its impact on the work effort of AFDC mothers. Chapter 5, "Work Requirements: WIN," examines the Work Incentive program's effect on the work-welfare choice of these mothers. No visible results came out of the 1967 attempts to promote work, so that proposals for "welfare reform," in effect a federal takeover of public assistance, were the next step.

Chapter 6, "Welfare Reform: From Work Incentives to Work Requirements," examines these proposals. Reform plans again utilized incentives and requirements to further the work goal but they were novel in other ways. They separated out the employables from the unemployables, literally creating two assistance groups: those who were able to maintain themselves and those who were not. Each group was to have a different type of assistance in accordance with this distinction. At the same time, employables who were not (yet) on assistance were to be included in the assistance provision. This twofold strategy insured that employables on welfare would work and hopefully go off welfare, and employables not on welfare would also work (and not go on welfare). The welfare reform proposals were not acceptable enough to Congress and so did not become law. Instead, the Talmadge amendment, which was a work requirement tacked on to the existing AFDC program, did become law and for the present is the only pertinent plan to contain the AFDC caseload through the mechanism of work.

Work or Welfare?

1

ANTECEDENTS OF
WORK AND WELFARE

MOTHERS' PENSIONS

In 1911 Illinois and Missouri passed the first state Mothers' Pensions laws, providing, for the first time, state governmental aid to children in their own homes. Before this, the children of widowed and other lone parents who were deprived of support were either sent to institutions or, in a small measure, assisted by private social agencies. By the turn of the century, institutional care had come under attack as being too costly and also detrimental to the welfare of these children. It was agreed that another form of assistance had to be found, but the question of whether relief should be public or private resulted in a virtual battle between the proponents and the opponents of state Mothers' Pensions.

The Charity Organization Society and other voluntary agencies opposed public sponsorship. They felt this would ensure assistance as a "right" rather than as a privilege and from this conception disastrous results would follow. Many families who were morally and financially undeserving of assistance would, without the close and personal scrutiny of private philanthropy, be indiscriminately aided. Public relief would become like poor relief--corrupt and pauperizing. The huge numbers of recipients drawn in by such promiscuous methods of giving would bankrupt the treasury. And finally, without a careful selection of recipients who could benefit from "constructive" supervision, the necessary rehabilitation of the client would not be possible.

The advocates of Mothers' Pensions, on the other hand, saw assistance to children deprived of parental support as a "right"--a payment to widows and others for services

1

rendered to the state, these services being the care and up-
bringing of their own children, who were future citizens of
the state. Since large numbers of children were in need as
a result of this condition and all should be served, the taxpayer should finance this endeavor through public auspices.

The different assistance philosophies inherent in the
public and private conceptions of aid to children reflected
an essential dichotomy in relief ideology. The adherents of
private aid modeled their preferences on the practices of
the Charity Organization Societies. These had given individualized assistance to selected fatherless families that
entailed moral and practical supervision; the seeking out of
any available resources from friends, relatives, and the
mother's own efforts; and small supplementary grants. The
idea of pensions for children deprived of parental support
(mostly through the father's death) was based on assistance
given by virtue of status (fatherless children) to a large
group. In theory it meant little means testing, no supervision, and flat grants adequate to fulfill the purpose of
raising children in their own homes. In the first instance,
private charity made a "contract" with the mother to give
her some assistance in return for which she would make every
effort to help herself; this, of course, usually meant work
for the mother. A pension grant, on the other hand, in essence required from the mother only that she bring up her
children properly; this meant that she remain at home in
order to do this.

The private social agencies were thwarted despite their
efforts to prevent Mothers' Pensions and by 1915, 23 states
had initiated such legislation. By 1921, 40 states had made
this provision, and in 1935 pensions for mothers existed in
all but two states--Georgia and North Carolina. Apparently
the states had realized the "contribution of the unskilled
or semi-skilled mothers in their own homes exceeded their
earnings outside of the home and that it was in the public
interest to conserve their child-caring functions."[1] Although the proponents of pensions had won the debate over
public and private aid, state Mothers' Pensions programs
did not adhere to a pension assistance philosophy. Once
pensions became a reality, workers from the voluntary agencies succeeded in taking over the administration of these
programs. As a result, practice became infused with Charity
Organization methods and goals.

In consonance with these methods and goals was the fact
that Mothers' Pensions always remained a small program. By
1930, only 256,000 children in 31 states were beneficiaries.
Although by 1934 all but three states had such a provision,
even where it was operative, the pensions were in many

places "optional to the local sub-division responsible for their administration."[2] The clientele was not only few in numbers, it was comprised only of "deserving" families. Mothers were selected for the grant for their moral fitness and the suitability of the home. So unique were these mothers supposed to be that Winifred Bell notes, "the mere act of receiving a Mothers' Pension grant bestowed prestige, so high were the moral and child-rearing expectations."[3] Though most state legislation included abandoned, separated, and divorced mothers, in practice the mother was a widow in 82 percent of the families in 1931, and in New York State as many as 88 percent were widows.[4] In the southern states, according to Robert Lansdale, "Negroes were substantially excluded from these programs."[5]

The "high level" of the families served did not result in equally high or even adequate grants. They averaged from $4.33 to $69.31 monthly per family, with the lower amounts falling in the southern states.[6] In theory the grants were to be high enough to allow the mother to stay at home and care for her children:

> In practically all of the states the legislation explicitly or implicitly provides that the grant shall be sufficient . . . to maintain the family at a reasonable standard of living in order that the mother may not be under the necessity of outside employment and thus neglect her children.[7]

However, Grace Abbott and others pointed out that this theory was often violated in practice. In many states the payment was so low that the grant was, in fact, "only supplemental relief, and the mother worked outside the home."[8]

Supervision in Mothers' Pensions was similar to what it was in the voluntary giving of the Charity Organization Societies. It aimed to rehabilitate the family to self-support. Toward this goal, the mother had to avail herself of every possible resource, be it through solicitation of aid from friends and relatives or through her own (or her children's) work. Assistance was seen as a "last resort" and used to supplement other sources of income. Another supervisory goal was direction in the care of children. The two goals of self-support and child care were in conflict, and the tension between them was expressed in some ambivalence whether and to what degree the mother should work.

Was the mother in fact free to stay at home and afford high-level care to her children in light of the small stipend and the onus upon her to become self-maintaining? One attempt to resolve this dilemma consisted of permitting (or encouraging) her to work part of the time when substitute care was available; another had the mother doing work at home, such as laundry. Blanche Coll explains that "assistance payments were universally so low that many recipients worked as domestics, took in laundry or performed other unskilled work. In the middle of the prosperous twenties, maximum grants allowed in the various states were at subsistence or less than subsistence level."[9] These select recipients of mothers' aid did in fact perform a great deal of work. In Pennsylvania, 75 percent of a group of 116 mothers were employed in 1918. In 1923 over 50 percent of a sample of 942 mothers in nine metropolitan areas were working, and as many as 69 percent in Westchester County, New York.[10]

In Mothers' Pensions, the charity philosophy prevailed over the concept of pension assistance. Relief was therefore seen as supplemental to other income and not substitutive for it; mothers were thus encouraged to make every possible effort to become self-maintaining. Low grants and insecure payments made to selected recipients who could benefit from a type of supervision that elicited independence resulted in work for these mothers. The same conflict of interests was to emerge again in Aid to Dependent Children.

SOCIAL SECURITY

During the Depression, the lack of available work created an atmosphere in which individual fault as a cause of poverty was not feasible and in which the federal government saw its role as that of preventing destitution. The Federal Emergency Relief agencies (FERA) were created to dispense relief to huge numbers of those unemployed as a result of the Depression. In 1935 the national unemployment rate was as high as 32 to 40 percent. President Roosevelt terminated the FERA and created the Works Progress Administration, which was in essence a high-level work-relief program "for saving the lives, health, and in part the skills and self-respect, of millions of citizens."[11] To Harry Hopkins and others at the time, "work relief seemed highly preferable to dole-oriented programs."[12]

But Roosevelt was also concerned with preventing the results of another catastrophic depression in the future. To this end, he created a Committee on Economic Security to recommend legislation that would cushion the risks of industrialization. Unemployment Compensation for employables out of work, Old Age Insurance, and Old Age Assistance (the latter a public assistance program for the aged) were the prime focus of both the president and the Committee on Economic Security. A continuing provision for work-relief called "employment assurance" also was recommended.

The basic public assistance program being proposed was Old Age Assistance (OAA). Aid to the Blind (AB) was added later in Congress. It was only through the insistence of the Children's Bureau (the agency that had supervised state Mothers' Pensions) which had representation on the Citizens' Advisory Council (to the Committee on Economic Security), that Aid to Dependent Children became one of the public assistance titles. This Advisory Council was largely composed of social workers, like those who had manned the Mothers' Pensions programs; in fact, Katherine Lenroot and Martha Elliot of the Children's Bureau had been instrumental in drafting the ADC proposal.[13]

When the Social Security proposal reached Congress, Unemployment Compensation and the Old Age Insurance programs were vigorously debated, but little controversy ensued over ADC, which together with Old Age Assistance and Aid to the Blind were viewed as the public assistance programs for <u>unemployables</u>. ADC was, in fact, considered the least important of the three: federal participation was limited to one-third of expenditures here, while OAA and AB enjoyed a "one-half" status. As with Mothers' Pensions, the mother was not included in the grant, but seen only as the "caretaker" of the children, who were the beneficiaries.

The continuing "employment assurance" that the Committee on Economic Security had recommended did not appear in the Social Security Act. No work requirements were attached to Title IV (ADC), nor, however, were any restrictions put upon the states as to requirements <u>they</u> may choose to put on ADC recipients. Though Congress saw this program as being for unemployables, it was not appropriate federal business to legislate this intent, nor did they deem it necessary. The statement of the Senate Finance Committee that the ADC program was for those children who were "in relief families which will not be benefited through work programs or the revival of industry"[14] seemed sufficient to attest to the congressional image of Aid to Dependent Children as a provision for those outside the labor force.

Although the final designation of ADC as a public assistance program for unemployables was clearly in line with congressional intent, where the program should be placed evolved only after some debate. The Committee on Economic Security had recommended that ADC be under the jurisdiction of the Federal Emergency Relief Agency, while the Children's Bureau had all along assumed that <u>it</u> would administrate ADC.

Had the program gone to the FERA, an agency whose task had
been relief for employables, the definition of a deprived
child would have been of one living in a family where there
is "no adult person . . . who is able to work and provide
the family" with support. This could have been taken to
mean that either one or both parents are present and unemployed; the reasons for aid would then have included unemployed but employable parents. Had ADC come under the aegis
of the Children's Bureau, it would have had the earmarks of
the Mothers' Pensions programs in terms of selectivity of
clientele and rehabilitative counseling toward the goal of
self-maintenance. As it was, Congress created an independent agency--the Social Security Board--that located ADC in
a more neutral, less employment-oriented setting, together
with the programs for other unemployables (the aged and the
blind).

The final definition of a deprived child as amended in
the Senate under the influence of the Children's Bureau contained the requirement that the parent be "dead, disabled,
or absent" (words taken directly from the texts of the state
Mothers' Pensions laws) and not in any case "unemployed."
It legislatively marked the program as one for children
whose parent was not able to provide support because he or
she was outside the labor market, and it put the program
into a public assistance framework. While the Children's
Bureau administration would have meant contractual assistance and the FERA temporary relief for the unemployed, the
Social Security Board came closest to a pension type of aid.
At least in theory, this population was, like the blind and
the aged, entitled to aid on the basis of status only.

In line with this theory, Congress should have provided
for adequate grants to meet the full needs of families that
were afflicted by the "no fault" loss of a breadwinner. Instead (probably due less to ambivalence than to negligence),
it stipulated less federal financial participation to ADC
than to the other programs. Even more telling, Congress
chose to avoid the issue of benefits altogether. The original draft of the Social Security Act had included the tenet
that deprived children should be assisted at the level of "a
reasonable subsistence compatible with health and decency."
This was defeated by the southern senators, who feared that
giving high benefits to their Negro work force would erode
incentives and force wages up. The states were then left to
decide at what level they would assist ADC families. As a
result, benefits were abysmally low before the 1960s, both
nationally and especially in the southern states. In 1940
the national average monthly payment per family was only
$32.39; the low of $13.63 was in Alabama. Even by as late

as 1954, the average was $80.24, while the low in Mississippi was $26.20.[15] The low benefits apparently had their intended effect in the south, where from the beginning ADC recipients performed more work than anywhere else in the country.

The Social Security Act was passed in 1935 and included Title IV: Aid to Dependent Children. Although the act clearly defined a deprived child, nowhere did it mention the manner in which the states were to determine financial eligibility for the program. By 1939 the federal Social Security Board became apprehensive because some states were giving flat-rate pensions rather than relief to their old age assistance recipients; it thus became instrumental in amending the public assistance titles of the act to specify a means test that stipulated that "the State agency shall, in determining need, take into consideration any other income and resources of any child claiming aid to dependent children."

In its 1941 Annual Report, the board reiterated that "the purpose of these amendments is to insure that the State agency shall give consideration to all relevant facts necessary to an equitable determination of need and amount of assistance. Public assistance is intended to supplement rather than replace any available or continuing income and resources."[16] This dictum clearly prevented public assistance from becoming a "flat grant" pension and emphasized both the degree of need and the resource-obtaining potential of the recipient family. In so doing, it left the way open for a later emphasis on work as a way of increasing the latter and reducing the former, although ostensibly these recipients were outside the labor market. In a 1954 essay, "To Work or Not to Work," Elizabeth De Schweinetz, a Department of Health, Education and Welfare (HEW) consultant, justifies work for ADC mothers on the basis of this philosophy:

> The ADC program is not threatened if some
> mothers are required to work. ADC is a form
> of public assistance not an allowance to
> children or a mothers' pension. It is in-
> tended to meet economic need only when this
> need cannot be met by the actual or potential
> resources of the individual; and considera-
> tion of employment of the mother as a possible
> resource can be constructive if properly
> safeguarded.[17]

In its early years, the ADC program, in addition to paying low benefits, reached a small amount of children (only 20 per 1,000 children under age 18 were recipients in 1940).[18] Those it did reach were mainly the children of "deserving" parents. Three-fifths of the states in 1948 had "suitable home" policies. These policies, according to Bell, were fostered by the Social Security Board and favored by "prevailing professional opinion," and served to minimize the assistance given to the unmarried mother and to the Negro family. Between 1937 and 1940, only 14 to 17 percent of all recipients were Negro. In the south, they were even further underrepresented, comprising 12 percent of the caseload in Georgia, while 38 percent of the children in that state were Negro. Unmarried-mother families fared no better. In 1937, only 3.5 percent of all ADC children had an unmarried mother; five states had no families with unmarried mothers on ADC.[19]

Though the suitable home concept enabled states to deny assistance to Negroes, additional underlying motives were equally concerned with work. Public assistance agencies "could see no reason why the employable Negro mother should not continue her usually sketchy seasonal labor rather than receive a public assistance grant. They had always gotten along."[20] Where Negro women traditionally worked in agriculture, seasonal welfare policies were created to ensure continuation of the practice. In Louisiana, policy in 1943 required "all applicants or recipients of ADC to be refused assistance so long as they were needed in the cotton fields."[21] In Georgia and Arkansas a "farm policy" adopted in the early 1950s required that mothers take employment whenever it was available. In Arkansas from 40 to 60 percent of ADC case closings between 1953 and 1960 were due to this policy.[22]

The official federal attitudes toward work for ADC mothers in the beginning years of the program seem to have been liberal, at least if judged by policy statements of the Social Security Board. The Handbook of Public Assistance in 1946 advised that ADC should "make it possible for a mother to choose between staying at home to care for her children and taking a job away from home."[23] In 1950 the official position opposed "any policy of denying or withdrawing aid to dependent children as a method of bringing pressure upon women with young children to accept employment."[24]

The federal agency, however, did not constrain the states from instituting work requirements, and many did. In 1950 the State Plans for ADC in Arizona, Washington, D.C., Illinois, and Nebraska called for the parent to accept suitable employment if care was available for the children.[25] By 1953, ten State Plans contained this stipulation.[26] States, of course, could require this without it appearing in their State Plans. For example, Michigan in 1948 reduced the welfare grant by an amount equal to the earnings the mother would make in any job offered to her, whether or not she was actually working. This was quali- fied, however, by the mother's need to have the prerequi- sites for the job and by the availability of suitable child care.[27]

To what extent states actually enforced their require- ments is not clear. An HEW report written in 1961 states that seven states assumed income and budgeted "potential earnings from any parent who refused available employment." The author goes on to note that this was how these states tried to encourage employment. "These states did not spec- ify conditions under which employment was assumed to be available; however, one may well doubt the practicality of workers operating under the conditions set out in the pol- icy."[28] Charles Schottland, too, in 1963 wrote that 17 states had work requirements, but "in practice, most states do not enforce the requirement in the case of mothers with young children."[29] The southern states were said to have implemented work requirements to a substantial degree, while in other parts of the country, even where formal require- ments existed, great precautions were taken not to injure the family well-being. For example, Wisconsin state policy, while permitting the counties to "require the mother to do such remunerative work as in its judgement she can do with- out detriment to her health or the neglect of her children or her home," also directs that the following factors be considered: the effect of the father's death, disability or absence on the family; the prior role of the father; the prior functioning of the mother; the work history, apti- tudes, and motivation of the mother in relation to work; the mental and physical health of the mother; the emotional and social needs of the mother and children; the availabil- ity of child care.[30]

Whether work was compelled through administrative de- mand or a result of personal choice, a great deal of work was done by ADC mothers in the first 25 years of the pro- gram. In 1942 a review of family income in seven states showed that 40 percent of the income these families had was from earnings.[31] A study of six states by the Social Secu- rity Board in 1941 revealed that out of 338 families, 91 mothers (27 percent) worked.[32] In 1942 another official report indicates that in eight states, proportions of work- ing mothers ranged from 5 percent in Massachusetts to 47 percent in Arkansas,[33] and that 23 percent of the mothers in 16 states were designated as "unemployed or with insuf- ficient earnings." The author, interpreting this data, comments:

> The great range among states in the proportion
> of mothers who were reported as unemployed or
> with insufficient earnings indicates that the
> practices in some States encourage many moth-
> ers who would be considered as needed in the
> home in other states to supplement the family
> income by working. Undoubtedly the smallness
> of the assistance payment has forced some of
> these mothers to accept employment.[34]

Differences in administrative practices and in benefit levels apparently accounted for differences in work effort
among states--with more work effort produced where requirements were stringent and grants low. American Public Welfare Association surveys of national samples of ADC families
in 1950 and in 1960 both reveal that as much as 30 percent
of the mothers were at work during those years.[35]
    Aid to Dependent Children, as part of the 1935 Social
Security Act, was legislatively conceived as a pension-type
program for children who were deprived of support by the
loss of a breadwinner; as such, their families were viewed
as being outside the labor market. Through the influence
of the federal administrative agency, the Social Security
Board, the act was soon amended to insure that family resources be taken into account and the payment based on need
in addition to (deprived) status. This changed the nature
of the program to one that provided supplementary aid to
other resources; it left the way open for states to institute work requirements to make it possible for mothers to
obtain those resources. At the same time, as benefit levels
were left to the states by the federal legislation, the
states established low benefits, especially in the south.
Since the "reasonable subsistence" clause was deleted from
the federal legislation, the states could also pay less
than what they established as full need to recipients and
thus were able to disregard income from work between what
they were paying and what the family was said to need. Administrative work requirements, low benefits, and the low
"tax rate" option (exercised mainly in the south) produced
a sizable workforce of ADC mothers.

THE 1962 AMENDMENTS

By 1960 Aid to Dependent Children was no longer a program for small numbers of white widows and their children.
As many as 35 children under 18 years of age per 1,000 such
children in the general population were in receipt of those
benefits.[36] Whereas in 1940 the father was absent from the

10

home in 30 percent of ADC cases, by 1960 this was 64 percent. The proportion of widows decreased from 41 percent in 1940 to 8 percent of the number of children aided.[37] The costs of the program had been rising rapidly since the mid-1950s, due to greater numbers of recipients (a little over 1 million in 1940 and 3 million in 1960)[38] and to higher benefit levels (average monthly payment per recipient was $9.65 in 1940 and $27.45 in 1960).[39]

Moreover, ADC families were exhibiting "problem behavior." Desertion, child neglect, and delinquency were the concerns of the day and could be traced in preponderance to those families in the program. It was discovered in 1951 that a small proportion of the poor were absorbing a large proportion of social welfare resources, and in professional jargon these became known as the multiproblem or "hard-to-reach" families. Urban anthropologists like Walter B. Miller were describing this population in terms of a "culture of poverty," an epithet that was applied to the recipients of Aid to Dependent Children.

Attempts on the part of state administrations to stem the welfare tide growing both in numbers and in family disorganization resulted in battles as in Newburgh, N.Y. over fraud and in Louisiana over the wholesale rejection of public assistance clients and applicants through "suitable home" policies. The professionals who were involved in the administration of ADC were becoming open to charges of laxity and leniency.

In 1961 an ad hoc committee was formed consisting of two dozen professionals and headed by Wilbur Cohen (assistant secretary of HEW) to advise the administration on policy matters relating to public assistance. The committee's recommendations were heavily weighted in the direction of "services" for ADC families toward the goals of prevention and rehabilitation. Charles Gilbert classifies "Newburgh's effect on the Committee's deliberations" as explicit: "services, research and training were means of countering the assertion that fraud and laxity in public welfare stemmed from professional social work with the more realistic argument that they reflected insufficient professionalism."[40] The 1962 amendments, largely based on these recommendations, were proposed as a panacea for the rising rolls and the changing clientele of the ADC program.

The main tenet of the 1962 amendments was services, and the purpose of these services as stated in the Social Security Act was "to help maintain and strengthen family life and to help such parents or relatives to attain or retain capability for the maximum self-support and personal independence consistent with the maintenance of continuing

parental care and protection." President Kennedy, when he
signed the bill, said it was "to prevent or reduce dependency and to encourage self-care and self-support--to maintain family life where it is adequate and to restore it
where it is deficient."[41] Abraham Ribicoff, secretary of
HEW, pointed to the two objectives that new welfare legislation must address itself to: "eliminating whatever abuses
have crept into these programs and developing more constructive approaches to get people off assistance and back into
useful roles in society."[42] According to Irene Lurie, "congressional committees accepted the bill as a method of reducing welfare costs."[43]

Out of the mélange of aims inherent in the amendments,
two broad interests can be extracted: that of strengthening
family life and that of moving recipients of AFDC toward
self-support. The former was a response to allegations of
fraud, child neglect, delinquency, and desertion and resulted
in the professional solution of rehabilitation. The self-
support feature was addressed to growing rolls and rising
costs in an effort to reduce public dependency. Whether
these two interests were compatible, and whether the "services" strategy could bridge the gap between them, was problematic.

In 1956 the Social Security Act had been amended to
include the provision of services for the first time. The
same purposes--"self-care, self-support, and strengthening
family life" as enacting the views of the Department of
Health, Education and Welfare and the profession of social
work--were expressed, but, according to Gilbert, "the 1956
amendments had little effect on the rendering of services."[44]
Services were left optional with the states and no financial
incentive was given for the states to provide them since
they were "inserted" for purposes of federal reimbursement
into the 50 percent matching formula accorded all other administrative activities.

Under the 1962 formula, certain services, if provided,
would afford the states the usual 50 percent matching; other
so-called prescribed services, if all offered by the state,
would yield 75 percent reimbursement from the federal government. A 1964 HEW publication refers to federal policies
that had emerged from the 1962 service amendments, and de-
fines the "50 percent" services as casework, community planning, group work, homemaker service, volunteer service,
foster care, and training for self-support or self-care.
"Seventy-five percent services," instead of being delineated
by service, are defined by groups to be serviced: all families with adults with potentials for self-support, all unmarried parents and their children with special problems,

12

all families disrupted by desertion, all children in need
of protection, all children with special problems.[45]

The first category, families with employable adults,
is defined, as "disabled or unemployed fathers and employable
mothers not needed in the home." The methodology for improving self-support potential is

> casework service to assess capacity for and,
> if appropriate, promote self-support; to re-
> move personal or family barriers to self-
> support and to encourage the adult to upgrade
> skills and to secure and maintain suitable
> employment; and the use of community re-
> sources for evaluation of employment poten-
> tials, vocational training, necessary medi-
> cal services, securing employment and for
> child care.[46]

The report goes on to say that "casework, including full use
of related community resources, and community planning are
the only service methods that are required in carrying out
the above services."

In addition to services, the 1962 amendments legislated
other work-related provisions. In 1961 the revolutionary
Unemployed-Parent (UP) amendment was added to the ADC Title
of the Social Security Act to supplement the "dead, disabled, or absent" definition of a deprived child by including an unemployed parent. The high level of unemployment
at that time, coupled with desertion as an ever-growing
reason for ADC eligibility, led to the hope that providing
relief to families with unemployed fathers would prevent
families from being left without a wage-earner. Corollary
to this goal was the plan that these fathers would be given
work and training while in receipt of ADC. This was mandatory: in order for a family to be eligible for ADC-UP, the
father must accept work. By 1962, the UP provision, which
had only been authorized for a year, was extended to 1967,
and Community Work and Training Programs (CWT) were also
initiated as part of the 1962 amendments. The father now
had to accept work and training (if offered) to be eligible
for the grant. This inclusion of evident employables into
the program for the first time led to the beginning of an
expressed federal interest in work for recipients of ADC.

The Social Security Act had to be amended to permit
federal reimbursement for the CWT programs in 1962. Section 409, which authorized CWT, changed the existing law for
a limited period of time (until June 30, 1967) and specified
certain safeguards that would ostensibly distinguish CWT,

13

defined as "work and training," from ordinary work-relief. These included provisions for health and safety measures, rates of pay not less than the state legal minimum, consideration of work expenses, and useful work that would serve a public purpose and would not displace regular workers; the worker was to have the opportunity to seek regular work or training; aid was not to be denied if the person refused to work with good cause; and child-care arrangements were to be assured.[47] Notwithstanding these fine procedural distinctions, the CWT provision with its emphasis on rehabilitation could be seen as carrying with it the onus of work-relief. Most important, it was, in fact, the forerunner of later efforts both to reform and restrain the Aid to Dependent Children population through the mechanism of work.

The 1962 amendments legislated the first two concrete incentives to employment. They stipulated that "earned or other" income could be disregarded in determining the amount of the grant if such income were to be "set aside" for the specific, identifiable future needs of the dependent children. The amendments also made mandatory the disregarding of work expenses in the computation of the ADC budget. Both of these earned income exemptions were included together in Section 106 of the amendments, which was entitled "Incentives for Employment Through Consideration of Expenses in Earning Income, and Provisions for Future Needs of Dependent Children." These were the first federal attempts to require the states to disregard portions of income from work in order to provide incentives for work, and thus established the policy (to be greatly expanded later) of offering rewards for work effort.

The 1962 amendments also increased the federal allotment for child welfare services in order to provide day care for the children of working AFDC parents. A redefinition of child welfare services was inserted to include in its purposes the function of "protecting and promoting the welfare of children of working mothers." Interestingly enough, this was not added to the ADC Title IV, but to Title V of the Social Security Act, which is concerned with child welfare services. The allocation of day care to Title V was not accidental and illustrated the tension between the two aims of day care: to provide care for children and to permit the mother to work; these further reflect the two principal goals of the 1962 amendments: strengthening family life and reducing dependency.

The services aspect of the 1962 amendments were not implemented to any substantive degree. The HEW publication of November 1964, reviewing a 21-month period after the amendment became effective, points out that 18 states

together had added only 50 full-time and 20 part-time staff
to carry out the service function, one state having added 3
of the 50 full-time workers. Seventeen states reported that
they had together only 287 specialists devoting 50 percent
of their time to social services. The same document attributes a reduction in the cost of assistance of $706,600 to
closed cases without specifying whether they were closed for
employment or how this figure compares with previous savings. It adds that "this emphasis [services] appears largely
responsible" for the closings, but also notes that in some
counties assistance costs increased "because either the
needs became better known or the agency raised its standards
of assistance to promote its social objectives more effectively."[48]

The 1967 national HEW statistics paint a somewhat more
positive picture of services rendered. According to that
account, as many as 80 percent of all AFDC families received
at least one type of service. The description of these services, however, modifies this optimistic estimate. "Health
care" is defined as a social service, with as much as 33
percent having had this benefit, although it is not clear
whether this refers to medical efforts by the welfare agency
or care through Medicaid or ordinary free clinic service.
Similarly, "protection of children" is a service given to
11.5 percent of the families, but referral to child protective agencies--probably what is being considered here--had
taken place in welfare offices long before the "service-
orientation" instituted by the 1962 amendments. Other services that would fall into the area of "strengthening family
life" are loosely defined as "improved family functioning,"
25.4 percent; "maintaining family life and improved family
functioning," 30.7 percent; "maintaining home," 17.5 percent; "maintaining or improving social relationships and
participation in community life," 8 percent. Self-support
services, also not specified, were given to only 8.6 percent
of all families.[49] It is difficult to see how these obscure
categories could be defined as specific services and how
their results could be measured.

Gilbert lists the reasons why, in his view, services
in ADC never quite became a reality: the 1962 amendments
did not actually define services, and neither was Congress
able to specify them. The problem of definition "was left
to the professionals." In the welfare agencies, operational
obstacles arose when it was not known whether to classify
recipients in terms of problems, methods, or services. The
lack of standards by which to allocate, measure, and evaluate services created problems. It was not clear how to
match a professional activity (casework) with the formal

requirements of vast, bureaucratically oriented public assistance agencies. The professional explanation was, afterward, expressed in terms of lack of sufficient professional staff to carry out the function.

The Community Work and Training programs fared no better than the service strategy. Less than 2 percent of adult AFDC recipients had taken part in the program at any one time.[50] In the latter two years of the program's existence, 1966 and 1967, only 15,333 AFDC families, or 1.2 percent, had a member enrolled in a CWT program.[51]

If the dual intent of services was to strengthen family life and reduce dependency, this was surely not carried out. The rate of illegitimacy in AFDC rose dramatically after 1962: in 1961, 21.3 percent of families had a father not married to the mother; in 1967 this was the case for 28.4 percent.[52] The proportion of families with divorced, separated, or deserted parents was 40.5 percent in 1961 and 43.5 percent in 1967.[53] Services did not appear to be effective, at least in preventing family break-up. Neither was dependency reduced as the number of recipients increased from over 3.5 million in 1961 to almost 5.5 million in 1967.[54]

From 1967 on it became acceptable to say that services were "sold" to Congress in 1962 as a means of reducing dependency. The promise and the failure of services to do so may, in fact, have led to much more stringent measures taken later on to effect this goal. The problem may lie in the discrepancy between the professional notion of the outcome of services and the congressional view. Social work and other helping professions were primarily concerned with the "health" of the individual. All therapeutic measures were intended to lead to this goal, and the strategy for achieving it was rehabilitation. If an individual could be rehabilitated (his or her "family life strengthened"), he would by definition become self-supporting. Public dependency would, therefore, be reduced.

The professionals, however, became fixated on the interim goals of "health," and Congress was less interested in promoting the psychological health of individuals than in reducing the taxpayers' burden of carrying growing welfare loads. Work, in professional ideology, was a sign of health, while work to the layman and the politician was a constriction of the welfare rolls. This dilemma is neatly illustrated in the 1964 HEW report, which talks about the implementation of the 1962 service amendments. Under "results" (of a demonstration project with "hard-to-reach" families done with a voluntary family service agency), the report states that "this joint project served to improve the diagnostic skill of workers and also improved the voluntary agency's understanding of public welfare." Another group-work project for AFDC mothers was initiated "for socialization and for group discussions about common concerns." Another result of services listed was "increased community interest in the welfare departments and better utilization of community resources."[55] These "results" were seen to be positive by professional standards, but would hardly be the concern of either Congress or the general public who wanted more concrete "results" than these.

NOTES

1. Grace Abbott, The Child and the State (Chicago: University of Chicago Press, 1938), p. 229.

2. Robert T. Lansdale, "The Impact of the Federal Social Security Act on Public Welfare Programs in the South," Research Reports in Social Science 4, no. 1 (February 1961): 30.

3. Winifred Bell, "Rejected Families: A Study of 'Suitable Home' Policies in Aid to Dependent Children" (Ph.D. dissertation, Columbia University School of Social Work, August 1964), p. 20.

4. Mother's Aid, 1931, Children's Bureau Publication No. 220 (Washington, D.C.: 1933).

5. Lansdale, op. cit., p. 38.

6. Winifred Bell, Aid to Dependent Children (New York: Columbia University Press, 1965), p. 14.

7. John Lewis Gillin, Poverty and Dependency (New York: Appleton-Century, 1937), p. 413.

8. Grace Abbott, From Relief to Social Security (Chicago: University of Chicago Press, 1941), p. 187.

9. Blanche D. Coll, Perspectives in Public Welfare, U.S. Department of Health, Education and Welfare (Washington, D.C., 1970), p. 79.

10. Bell, Aid to Dependent Children, op. cit., p. 16.

11. Charles McKinley and Robert W. Frase, Launching Social Security (Madison: University of Wisconsin Press, 1962), p. 164.

12. Ibid., p. 10.

13. Edwin E. Witte, The Development of the Social Security Act (Madison: University of Wisconsin Press, 1962), p. 164.

14. Social Security Amendments of 1971, U.S. Senate, Committee on Finance, Hearings (Washington, D.C., 1972), p. 1309b.

15. Lansdale, op. cit., p. 37.

16. Jacobus TenBroek and Floyd W. Matson, Hope Deferred (Berkeley and Los Angeles: University of California Press, 1959), p. 93.

17. Elizabeth De Schweinetz, "To Work or Not to Work," Child Welfare 32, no. 10 (December 1954): 8.

18. Trend Report: Graphic Presentation of Public Assistance and Related Data, U.S. Department of Health, Education and Welfare (Washington, D.C., 1969), p. 29.

19. Bell, Aid to Dependent Children, op. cit., pp. 33-35.

20. Ibid.

21. Ibid., p. 46.

22. Ibid., p. 107.

23. Alvin L. Schorr, "Problems in the ADC Program," Social Work 5, no. 2 (April 1960): 7.

24. Riley E. Mapes, "The Mother's Employment--Whose Decision in A.D.C.?" Public Welfare 8, no. 4 (April 1950): 76.

25. Characteristics of State Public Assistance Plans, U.S. Department of Health, Education and Welfare (Washington, D.C., 1950).

26. Characteristics of State Public Assistance Plans, U.S. Department of Health, Education and Welfare (Washington, D.C., 1953).

27. Gary Louis Appel, Effects of a Financial Incentive on AFDC Employment (Minneapolis: Institute for Interdisciplinary Studies, 1972), p. 6.

28. Agnes White, State Methods for Determining Need in the Aid to Dependent Children Program, U.S. Department of Health, Education and Welfare (Washington, D.C., 1961), pp. 23, 24.

29. Charles I. Schottland, The Social Security Program in the United States (New York: Appleton-Century-Crofts, 1963), p. 113.

30. Joel F. Handler and Ellen Jane Hollingsworth, The "Deserving Poor" (Chicago: Markham, 1971), pp. 137, 138.

31. "Characteristics and Incomes of Families Assisted by Aid to Dependent Children," Social Security Bulletin 9, no. 7 (July 1946): 20, 21.

32. Aid to Dependent Children, A Study in Six States, Social Security Board (Washington, D.C., 1941), p. 79.

33. Families Receiving Aid to Dependent Children, Social Security Board (Washington, D.C., 1942), p. 22.

34. Ibid., p. 39.

35. Gordon W. Blackwell and Raymond F. Gould, Future Citizens All (Chicago: American Public Welfare Association, 1952), p. 50; M. Elaine Burgess and Daniel O. Price, An American Dependency Challenge (Chicago: American Public Welfare Association, 1963), p. 250.

36. Trend Report, op. cit.

37. Ibid.

38. Ibid., p. 27.

39. Ibid., p. 33.

40. Charles E. Gilbert, "Policy-Making in Public Welfare," Political Science Quarterly 81, no. 2 (June 1966): 209.

41. Irene Lurie, "An Economic Evaluation of Aid to Families with Dependent Children" (Washington, D.C.: The Brookings Institution, 1968), p. 46 (mimeographed).

42. Public Assistance 1962, U.S. Department of Health, Education and Welfare (Washington, D.C., 1962), p. 2.

43. Lurie, op. cit., p. 45.

44. Gilbert, op. cit., p. 199.

45. Report on the Implementation and Results of the 1962 Service Amendments to the Public Assistance Titles, U.S. Department of Health, Education and Welfare (Washington, D.C., 1964).

46. Ibid., p. 2.

47. Public Welfare Amendments of 1962, U.S. Senate, Committee on Finance, Report (Washington, D.C., 1962), pp. 27, 28.

48. Report on the Implementation and Results, op. cit., p. 17.

49. Findings of the 1967 AFDC Study, U.S. Department of Health, Education and Welfare (Washington, D.C., 1970), Table 71.

50. Lurie, op. cit., p. 20.

51. Findings of the 1967 AFDC Study, op. cit., Table 77.

52. Characteristics of Families Receiving Aid to Families with Dependent Children, November-December 1961, U.S. Department of Health, Education and Welfare (Washington, D.C., 1963), Table 12; Findings of the 1967 AFDC Study, op. cit., Table 23.

53. Ibid.

54. Trend Report, op. cit., p. 27.

55. Report on the Implementation and Results, op. cit., pp. 17-19.

2

PATTERNS OF
WORK AND WELFARE

Only within the last few years has the employment of
AFDC mothers become an issue. When the AFDC program started
in 1935, most recipients were the children of widows and,
like its predecessor Mothers' Pensions, the program had the
explicit function of keeping the mother out of the labor
force and in the home to better raise her fatherless children. Early studies of AFDC indicate that the primary interest was the welfare or progress of AFDC children, who,
together with their widowed mothers, clearly comprised a
segment of the "deserving poor." In fact, the progress
made by children in recipient homes was attributed to the
beneficial effects of stable income from AFDC, and continuous periods of assistance were considered desirable for
their welfare.

But the AFDC family has changed since 1935. In 1950
the father was deceased in as few as 18 percent of the families; in 1961 in only 6.8 percent; and in 1967 in only 5.5
percent.[1] Similarly, in 1950 mothers who were divorced,
separated, deserted, or unmarried accounted for 37 percent
of the caseload; in 1961, 57 percent; and in 1967, 70 percent.[2]

In addition to the statistical signs of family "disorganization," AFDC families began demonstrating "problem
behavior." Bradley Buell in 1951 discovered that a small

This chapter is a revised version of an article that
appeared in Welfare in Review 9, no. 6 (November-December,
1971), U.S. Department of Health, Education and Welfare,
and was coauthored by Barbara Wishnov.

proportion of poor families were absorbing a large proportion of social welfare resources.[3] Elaine Burgess and Daniel Price in their 1960 study list child neglect, promiscuity, desertion, and alcoholism as behavioral problems among AFDC families, now known as multiproblem families.[4] Perhaps even more important than the change in the composition of the caseload was its growing size. The number of recipients increased, nationally, from 2 million in 1950, to 3 million in 1960, to over 9 million in 1970, and to over 10 million in (April) 1971.[5]

Over the years in the population at large, it has become more and more acceptable for women, including mothers, to work outside the home. In 1970, 43 percent of all U.S. women were in the labor force, as contrasted with only 38 percent in 1960.[6] The War on Poverty, branding poverty and dependency as undesirable states, offered jobs as the panacea to cure these ills and centered much attention on employment for public assistance recipients.

The 1967 amendments to the Social Security Act placed a work requirement on some AFDC recipients and authorized a cash incentive for employment (the first $30 earned per month by an AFDC mother could now be kept without the penalty of grant reduction, and an additional third of earned income could also be disregarded). The growing importance of work for both women and poor persons, coupled with an AFDC population that was growing both in numbers and family disorganization, apparently led to the Congress' interest in the employment of AFDC mothers.

A THEORY OF WORK AND WELFARE

Coupled with the original intent of the AFDC program that mothers not work is the pervasive belief that they, indeed, do not work. Although a national study conducted in 1950 uncovered a substantial work history for AFDC "caretakers," the data did little to change the image of a homebound mother who had never worked and who was and would forever be dependent on public assistance.

But as it became functional to think of AFDC women as more than homebound, it was discovered that such women work before, after, and while on public assistance. Martin Rein and S. M. Miller in 1968, drawing their data from two national studies, pointed out that AFDC women have a substantial work history even while receiving aid. They tied their finding to the idea of an "irregular economy of poverty areas" that provides mainly low-paid marginal, and part-time employment to slum dwellers and that dictates certain irregular patterns of employment. They concluded: "Public assistance often served as a form of wage supplementation for the low-paid, partially employed worker. Welfare status did not necessarily represent a sharp break with the labor force, as the theory of assistance would imply."[7]

Genevieve Carter, at about the same time, noted that some AFDC women used public assistance sporadically or episodically to substitute for the loss of other income, especially income from employment. She says that it is a mistake to think of these families (as had been done) as "spiraling downward through ever-increasing amounts of deterioration brought on by self-induced crises that lead to public assistance."[8] Instead, she says, they use welfare in conjunction with work at different times and in different ways, their actions being more reflective of an irregular job economy than of personal failure.

Empirical studies like Sydney Bernard's (1964) discovered that "AFDC operates as an important buttress to the labor market in providing income to a significant group of families who occupy the lowest level of occupational structure."[9] More recently (1970) Charles Valentine, who was studying 80 ghetto families intensively in a participant ethnographical study, suggested that

> under fluctuating and marginal economic conditions the actual sources of general subsistance and occasional surplus become multiple, varied, and rapidly shifting . . . a great many individuals manage to garner small increments of income from several or numerous different origins. . . . For most citizens it is impossible to receive an adequate income without combining both wages and welfare and other resources.[10]

THE WELFARE PATTERN

The image we get from these accounts is of an interlacing of work and welfare and other resources in the lives of the very poor to effect an unstable and irregular kind of income maintenance. But how does public assistance fit into this economic picture? If it is, indeed, used as an alternative or supplement to work in the irregular economy, this fact will be reflected in program statistics for case turnover (likely to be high), duration of periods of assistance (likely to be short), number of periods of assistance (likely to be large), and reasons for opening and closing cases. "The game of musical chairs played by new cases, previous cases that return, and cases that close for a while or for good, reflects the interaction of the welfare system with the unstable employment conditions of the irregular, dead-end job economy available to them."[11]

William Grigsby, in a study of Baltimore (1960-66), verifies this suspicion: in this six-year period, 28,000 different families had received AFDC, or 75 percent more families than had received it for a single year. Only 2,000 of these families were continuously on public assistance; 24,000 were on-again, off-again; and "nearly all of the 28,000 constituted a permanent population at risk."[12] Grigsby's findings are supported by those of a study conducted by Greenleigh Associates in Washington State in 1964 in which 75 percent of all cases had been opened and closed before their current period on AFDC.[13] A very recent study in New York City estimates that over half of the average monthly AFDC case closings in 1972 are expected to return to welfare, and as much as 40 percent of average monthly case openings are reopenings.[14] Even more startling, 30 percent of openings during nine months in 1972 were closed within one year, while 27 percent of closings were reopened within one year.[15]

National studies that are conducted at only one point in time and include rural as well as metropolitan areas (in the Washington study over 78 percent of the respondents were city dwellers)[16] show lower recidivist figures. In 1960 the Burgess and Price cross-country survey found that 36 percent of the families studied had received AFDC previously.[17] In 1961 the national study conducted by the U.S. Department of Health, Education and Welfare found that 33 percent of the current cases had been opened before;[18] in 1967, 39 percent;[19] in 1969, 38 percent,[20] and in 1971, 35 percent.[21] Nationally, therefore, at least a third of the AFDC caseload "turns over."

For this to be a viable pattern, recipients will have been receiving AFDC for short rather than long periods. In a 1950 national study, Gordon Blackwell and Raymond Gould found that 20 percent of AFDC cases had terminated within a year and 50 percent within two years; only 11 percent had been "on" seven years or more.[22] In 1960 Burgess and Price found that 23 percent of AFDC families had received AFDC for under two years, 40 percent for two or more years, and 12 percent for seven or more years.[23] The 1961 HEW national study reported that 31 percent of all AFDC families had received aid for less than a year and 16 percent for one to two years--thus, almost half fell into the category "under two years."[24] HEW's 1967 study found that 17 percent of the families had been on AFDC for six months since the most

recent opening, 18 percent for one year but less than two,
11 percent for two years but less than three, only 8 percent
between seven and ten years, and only 8 percent for over ten
years.[25] The 1967 Washington State study gives similar figures: 20 percent of AFDC recipients had been on less than
six months, 37 percent less than a year, 55 percent less
than two years, 79 percent less than five years, and 92 percent less than ten.[26] HEW's 1969 study lists 32 percent of
all AFDC families as having received assistance less than a
year and 51 percent less than two years.[27]

All figures show that persons receiving AFDC continuously for long periods of time comprise a very small part
of the total caseload. The old image of "forever dependent
families" has had to be modified to include periods of independence. The median length of time on public assistance
has centered on a two-year period since 1950, with very little variation. But short periods of assistance do not mean
that each family receives aid for one short period only. To
take the idea of interspersed periods of work and welfare
further, a proportion of the same families must go back and
forth from one to the other. This fact is reflected in data
on the number of case openings and closings or periods of
assistance for the same families.

The first major national effort to consider this issue
was the Burgess and Price study, which cited 19 percent of
its sample as having had one closing previous to the time
of the study, 7 percent two previous closings, 3 percent
three previous closings, and 4 percent four or more.[28] In
1961, 20 percent of the cases in the national sample had
been opened once before, 7 percent twice before, and 5 percent three or more times before.[29] Greenleigh Associates
found an even higher figure of previous openings; 24 percent had one previous opening, 11 percent two, 12 percent
three, 7 percent four, and as much as 20 percent five or
more.[30] Grigsby's findings, though put in a different cast,
are even more revealing. Of all the AFDC closings in Baltimore in 1960, 65 percent had been reopened by 1963. Of all
the 1963 closings, 35 percent were reopened within three
months.[31]

The part of the caseload that is in flux includes a
group of recipients who follow a pattern of going on and
off welfare. It is not equally clear what proportion of
these cases are opened or closed for reasons of employment.
Blackwell and Gould in 1950 show that 25 percent of their
sample of closed cases were closed because of the "employment or increased earnings of one or more (other than the
father) members of the family."[32] In 1960 Burgess and
Price cited 10 percent of their cases as having been closed

because of the "employment or increased earnings of the mother."[33] According to a 1969 HEW study, in the first half of that year 13.6 percent of closings were due to the mother's employment or increased earnings.[34]

These figures, though illuminating, do not tell the whole story. For example, in the Burgess and Price study, of the cases with insufficient income when AFDC ended, 17.5 percent of the mothers said they would try to get jobs.[35] In addition, reasons for closing cases (other than for employment) such as "absent-parent returned," "youngest child reached age 18," and "failure to comply with agency policy" do not indicate the future source of income of these families and may portend employment for the mother, especially when other alternatives fail. In other words, the feasibility of employment _after_ the case is closed, rather than exactly at the point of termination, is present, though this pattern does not show up in closing statistics.

Similarly, Greenleigh Associates give "loss of employment" as the reason for _opening_ cases in 10.6 percent of the cases they studied; but they also indicate that an additional 9.1 percent were opened because the mother was pregnant and 5.3 percent because of the "incapacity or illness of the homemaker."[36] Mothers may have been employed though they were pregnant or ill. HEW's national sample for January-June 1969 found that in 8.2 percent of the cases the reason for opening was "lay-off, discharge, or other reason" and in 9.4 percent "illness, injury or other impairment." Just over 10 percent of the cases were opened because the families were "living below agency standards"--a possible code for hidden employment.[37]

The only effort to connect caseload dynamics with reasons for case openings and closings was in the study completed in December 1973 by the Human Resources Administration of New York City. It found that of all the openings in AFDC for reasons of unemployment between January and September 1972, as much as 35 percent were closed within one year. Similarly, 22 percent of those that had been closed for employment reopened within one year.[38]

The pattern that emerges from these statistics indicates that there is a small group of "stable" AFDC families that uses welfare continuously and a large group that rotates between being on and off. The data also show that a certain number of cases are opened and closed for reasons of employment and that this number may be even larger than is apparent. There is no certain way of conclusively linking these two phenomena of "on and off welfare" and employment, given the current state of the data, but the assumption can well be made that at least a substantial number

25

of the rotating cases actually do or could fall into the
category of "opened and closed for reasons of employment."

THE WORK PATTERN

If the thesis is true that AFDC women work to a substantial extent and irregularly, studies that have considered this issue, however few they be, will illustrate it.
The Blackwell and Gould 1950 survey considered work both
before and during public assistance and found that half the
mothers had a "usual occupation" during the crisis period--
the time preceding application for AFDC. About 33 percent
were actually employed during the crisis period, 11 percent
full time, and 17 percent part time; 3 percent were "in
other employment status," that is, in sporadic work, which
might also be part time or full time or seasonal.[39] Some
of the changes that occurred between both periods were in
the full-time employment group, which decreased from 11 to
5 percent, and in the "other employment status" group, which
increased from 3 to 7 percent. But fully a third of the
mothers had worked at some time both before and during the
receipt of AFDC.[40]
The irregularity of the employment is attested to on
several counts. Of the mothers who worked full time during
both periods, only half worked throughout the period; the
other half worked only "most of the period." Similarly, in
the part-time category, only half worked throughout both
periods. Under "other employment status," an even greater
degree of irregularity is found. The fact that this kind
of employment--sporadic, either full or part time--increased
while on AFDC may indicate that public assistance is a supplementary benefit to this kind of work more often than to
regular work. The data indicate that "irregular employment
characterized many of these homemakers."[41]
The patterns of employment uncovered by Burgess and
Price in their 1960 study are almost identical: about half
of the AFDC "homemakers" worked regularly and about half
irregularly, both full and part time. In addition to actual
work, however, they found that 16 percent of the homemakers
said they had looked for employment and had not found it
during the AFDC period.[42]
Some changes occurring between both periods (before and
after public assistance) include these: the full-time component dropped from 13 to 9 percent of the total; of the
mothers who were working full time in a regular capacity before receiving AFDC, only 50 percent continued to be so employed during the receipt of AFDC; 10 percent started to

work "full time most of period"; about 10 percent worked
part time both regularly and irregularly; 6 percent went
into "other employment status"; and 26 percent stopped all
work.[43] Burgess and Price attribute these changes to either
of two possibilities: the mothers voluntarily reduced their
work loads to be at home or they lost their employment.

The other category that changed the most between the
periods was "other employment status"--the category with
the most irregular employment patterns. Here the reverse
happened. As in 1950, this category increased from 3 to 7
percent of the total. Of those who were originally in this
group, 44 percent still were and 46 percent were no longer
employed. The size of this group increased mainly through
the addition of former full-time workers and, to a smaller
extent, former part-time regular workers and unemployed
women.[44]

Though the same proportion of women (30 percent) both
before and while receiving AFDC had some work experience,
"other employment status" was the smallest of all work categories (2.7 percent) in the crisis period but the next to
largest (6.8 percent) during the receipt of AFDC. Only
"part-time most of the period" (an almost equally irregular
type of employment) was higher (8.7 percent).[45] Apparently,
highly irregular employment is consistent with the receipt
of AFDC and may help "round out" a welfare income, in addition to being used as an alternative to public assistance
during certain periods in the lives of welfare recipients.

The Washington State study shows that 8 percent of the
AFDC respondents had income from work, amounting to an average wage of $77 per month. Aside from legal support orders,
this was the source of most income for these recipients.[46]
More to the point is the employment pattern indicated by
the data on the length of time women had been on their last
jobs and in the labor market. It presents a picture of long
association with the labor market but short employment periods. Fully 52 percent had been on their last jobs for
less than six months, but only 9 percent had been in the
labor market for so short a period. Fully 60 percent had
been at their last jobs for less than a year, but only 15
percent had been in the labor market so short a time. A
full 43 percent had been in the labor market for five to ten
years or more, but only 7 percent had been at their last
jobs so long.[47] These data seem to show a pattern of discontinuous periods of work.

The 1967 study of AFDC mothers in New York City shows
that they had substantial work histories. About a third
had worked only before their first child was born, another
third had worked both before and after, and 22 percent had

27

worked after the first child was born. All in all, as many
as 85 percent had worked at some time, meaning that only 15
percent had never worked.[48] Although the work pattern was
not studied, the length of time worked was as follows: 9
percent had worked for under a year, 21 percent for one to
three years, 22 percent for three to six years, 20 percent
for six to ten years, and as many as 28 percent for over
ten years.[49] They had, indeed, a great deal of work experience. The data, however, do not illustrate the irregularity of this experience--whether it was part time, full
time, sporadic, seasonal, or even less regular. But if
these were current AFDC recipients, 85 percent of whom had
work experience and many of whom had ostensibly been on assistance at previous times, the confluence of work and public assistance patterns seems very likely.

Leonard Goodman's data are consistent with the hypothesis that one segment of recipients intersperses periods of
work and welfare. In his study of a national sample of over
11,000 respondents (active, closed, and ineligible AFDC
cases) during a 37-month period from 1965 to 1968, he found
a good deal of employment was interlaced with public assistance as either a concurrent or alternate form of income
maintenance. More than half the respondents had been at
work at some time during the three-year period. Only a
third of those who worked had received no public assistance,
another third had received AFDC during the entire working
period, and the remaining third had received assistance during part of the three-year period. For two-thirds of this
group, work and public assistance were combined in some way
to afford an income. Of those who had received public assistance throughout, two-thirds had not worked during this
time and the other third had worked varying numbers of
months. Nine percent of the latter group had worked during all 37 months. Furthermore, of the active cases, only
48 percent had had no periods of employment, 10 percent two,
and 5 percent three or more.[50]

This discontinuous work pattern may, in actuality, have
been even more irregular than is apparent. The study failed
to obtain information from the respondents regarding whether
they worked part time or full time during the months worked
and whether they worked during the entire month in question.
The fact that 31 percent of those who were working at the
time of the interview were working part time seems to indicate that the same may be true for the previous three years.
Goodman's interpretation of the data to mean "steady employment is uncharacteristic of the recent lives of most of
the respondents"[51] is consistent with the theoretical framework dealing with the use of work and welfare discussed

earlier. His study also found that respondents had periods
of neither work nor public assistance nor husband's support
as a means of maintenance. Valentine's statement comes to
mind--people living under marginal economic conditions acquire small amounts of income from different sources and
the "actual sources of general subsistence and occasional
surplus become multiple, varied, and rapidly shifting."[52]

IMPLICATIONS

Public assistance policy since 1967 condones and en-
courages work for AFDC mothers. However, in contrast to
the image of AFDC women as a continuously dependent, never-
working group, patterns of work do exist and some form of
attachment to the labor force is present in most cases. The
nature of this attachment is tenuous, and the kinds of jobs
are different from those usual for most working people. The
jobs may be intermittent or seasonal or part time or afford
a few days a week of work or a few hours here and there.
Such jobs require little skill and, probably, in most instances yield little pay.

Because of its irregularity, attachment to this kind
of job market almost dictates a certain flexibility in disclosure. Jobs of this kind are difficult to report and ad-
vantageous to keep hidden (aside from the obvious benefit
of unbudgeted income, there is also the "plus" of no deductions). If this group, because it is caught in a fluctuating economy, accumulates small amounts of income from various sources, incomplete disclosure of resources and amount
of work would be consistent with this aim.

From the vantage point of the welfare system, work is
to be encouraged, and certain incentive features have been
incorporated into the budgeting procedure as a result of
the 1967 amendments (described earlier). This, coupled with
certain benefits in-kind such as food stamps and Medicaid,
has brought the public assistance payment to the point
where it is competitive with wages, especially the low wages
paid by the low-skilled job market. As a result, the incentive system has made it even more difficult for recipients
to "work themselves off welfare." The proportion of AFDC
women who are both at work and receiving public assistance
at the same time (overtly) has remained the same since 1967,
and case closings for employment have not increased.

Any effort to propel AFDC mothers toward employment
will have to make provision for jobs offering wages that
compete with "work and welfare." They will have to be regular enough, steady enough, and yield enough pay to override

some of the secondary benefits inherent in present ways of coping with income maintenance such as flexibility to move between work and welfare, the security of welfare payments, the potential for incomplete disclosure of resources, and minimal demands of irregular type jobs. Employment policy may also have to take into account elements of recipient life styles that are related to present means of income retrieval and that may be initially recalcitrant to new and different job opportunities.

NOTES

1. The AFDC program has declined from being the most important program supporting orphans to the least. For a study of this subject, see David B. Eppley, "Decline in the Number of AFDC Orphans: 1935-1966," Welfare in Review, September-November 1968, pp. 1-7.

2. Gordon W. Blackwell and Raymond F. Gould, Future Citizens All (Chicago: American Public Welfare Association, 1952), p. 21; Characteristics of Families Receiving Aid to Families with Dependent Children, November December 1961, U.S. Department of Health, Education and Welfare (Washington, D.C., 1963), Table 33; Findings of the 1967 AFDC Study, U.S. Department of Health, Education and Welfare (Washington, D.C., 1970), Table 22.

3. Bradley Buell and Associates, Community Planning for Human Services (New York: Columbia University Press, 1952).

4. M. Elaine Burgess and Daniel O. Price, An American Dependency Challenge (Chicago: American Public Welfare Association, 1963), p. 139.

5. Public Assistance Statistics, April 1971, U.S. Department of Health, Education and Welfare (Washington, D.C., 1971).

6. Statistical Abstract of the United States, U.S. Department of Commerce (Washington, D.C., 1970), p. 213.

7. Martin Rein, Social Policy: Issues of Choice and Change (New York: Random House, 1970), p. 304.

8. Genevieve W. Carter, "The Employment Potential of AFDC Mothers," Welfare in Review 6, no. 4 (July-August 1968): 1.

9. Sydney E. Bernard, "The Economic and Social Adjustment of Low-Income Female-Headed Families" (unpublished Ph.D. thesis, Brandeis University, 1964), p. 168.

10. Charles A. Valentine, "Blackston: A Progress Report on a Community Study in Urban Afro-America," study sponsored by the National Institute of Mental Health, U.S.

Department of Health, Education and Welfare (February 1970), pp. 19, 23 (mimeographed).

11. Carter, op. cit., p. 1.

12. William G. Grigsby, Possible Impacts of the Guaranteed Annual Income on Housing (Philadelphia: University of Pennsylvania Press, 1969), p. 8.

13. Greenleigh Associates, Poverty-Prevention or Perpetuation (New York: Greenleigh Associates, 1964), p. 34.

14. The Dynamics of New York City's Welfare Caseload, Human Resources Administration, City of New York (New York, November 1973), pp. 58, 59.

15. "The Quarterly Data Report of the Office of Policy Research" (New York: Human Resources Administration, July-September 1973), Tables II-7, II-8.

16. Greenleigh Associates, op. cit., p. 20.

17. Burgess and Price, op. cit., p. 48.

18. Characteristics of Families Receiving AFDC, op. cit., Table 6.

19. Findings of the 1967 AFDC Study, op. cit., Table 12.

20. Preliminary Report of Findings--1969 AFDC Study, U.S. Department of Health, Education and Welfare (Washington, D.C., 1970), Table 10.

21. Findings of the 1971 AFDC Study, U.S. Department of Health, Education and Welfare (Washington, D.C., 1971), Table 13.

22. Blackwell and Gould, op. cit., p. 38.

23. M. Elaine Burgess, "Poverty and Dependency: Some Selected Characteristics," Journal of Social Issues 21, no. 1 (January 1965): 85.

24. Characteristics of Families Receiving AFDC, op. cit., Table 4.

25. Preliminary Report of Findings--1969 AFDC Study, op. cit., Table 9.

26. Greenleigh Associates, op. cit., p. 34.

27. Preliminary Report of Findings--1969 AFDC Study, op. cit., Table 9.

28. Burgess and Price, op. cit., based on Table XIV, p. 257.

29. Characteristics of Families Receiving AFDC, op. cit., Table 6.

30. Greenleigh Associates, op. cit.

31. Grigsby, op. cit.

32. Blackwell and Gould, op. cit., p. 41.

33. Burgess and Price, op. cit., p. 56.

34. Reasons for Opening and Closing Public Assistance Cases, U.S. Department of Health, Education and Welfare (Washington, D.C., 1969), p. 9.

35. Burgess and Price, op. cit., p. 57.

36. Greenleigh Associates, op. cit., p. 30.

37. <u>Reasons for Opening and Closing Public Assistance Cases</u>, op. cit., p. 4.

38. "The Quarterly Data Report of the Office of Policy Research," op. cit.

39. Blackwell and Gould, op. cit., p. 56.

40. Ibid., p. 50.

41. Ibid., p. 57.

42. Burgess and Price, op. cit., p. 27.

43. Ibid., p. 250.

44. Ibid.

45. Ibid.

46. Greenleigh Associates, op. cit., p. 29.

47. Ibid., p. 39.

48. Lawrence Podell, <u>Families on Welfare in New York City</u> (New York: City University of New York, 1967), p. 25.

49. Ibid., p. 29.

50. Leonard H. Goodman, <u>Welfare Policy and its Consequences for the Recipient Population</u>, U.S. Department of Health, Education and Welfare (Washington, D.C., 1969), pp. 110-15.

51. Ibid.

52. Valentine, op. cit.

3

DETERMINANTS OF THE
WORK-WELFARE CHOICE

The increasing AFDC rolls from 1960 to 1972 have given rise to an interest in alternatives to welfare. Until recently, public assistance was seen as an income-maintenance means of "last resort"--a necessity to be drawn upon when all other alternatives had failed. A contending and more current view asserts that there is an element of choice in the use of welfare. This concept is based on the notion that there are competing ways for low-income families to manage their maintenance function; welfare is only one of these ways, and work is another. Congress, too, has taken this view and therefore in 1967 instituted a budgetary incentive for AFDC mothers, which disregards the first $30 per month in earnings and one-third of earnings thereafter.

On the assumption that it is possible to make a choice between work and welfare or some combination of the two, this chapter attempts to summarize some of the fragmented data available on the nature and determinants of the choice. Many possible factors may affect the work-welfare choice for AFDC women. This chapter is concerned with labor-force, monetary, and cultural determinants. Obviously, the labor-market structure, its job opportunities, and its income yields are of prime importance, but these will not be dealt with here as a class of determinants. They should be kept in mind as a backdrop or "given" upon which all other determinants impinge.

This chapter is a revised version of an article that appeared in Social Service Review, 46, no. 4 (December 1972).

It is relevant to note that a decision about work and welfare may not necessarily be made consciously and with full knowledge of all the factors bearing on the outcome. Moreover, no direct causal link from the variable to the individual's behavior is posited. The concern is rather with the general influences in the structure of the work situation, in the economics of welfare income, and in the culture or subculture that have a bearing on the aggregate behavior of low-income people.

LABOR-FORCE DETERMINANTS

The first area that recommends itself as significantly determinant of whether low-income mothers without male breadwinners will choose to work, to use welfare, or to do both is the concrete, pertinent job-relevant situation that such a woman may find herself in. The set of work-related characteristics that she possesses may, indeed, be a primary vantage point for her and may form the basis of her decision. Two such characteristics are her work history and her education and skill.

Work History

Just a few years ago the mother receiving AFDC was viewed as completely detached from the labor force. It is now known that most such women have substantial work histories. In the Burgess and Price national study of 1960, it was found that 30 percent of AFDC mothers had been working just before the receipt of AFDC.[1] Lawrence Podell's sample in New York City showed that eight out of ten such mothers had had work experience.[2] Leonard Goodman's data on 11,000 active, closed, and ineligible cases during 1965-68 noted that more than half the respondents had been employed at some time during the period.[3] The 1969 Department of Health, Education and Welfare survey verified that fully 61 percent of the mothers had been employed previously.[4]

In addition to working before and after assistance, a large number of women work while receiving assistance. The national HEW estimate of the proportion of female AFDC recipients at work in 1961, 1967, 1969, and 1971 remained at about 14 percent.[5] This proportion may be low since it reflects certain points in time rather than a cumulative period. It is not known to what extent this figure represents persons continually combining work and welfare and those working and receiving assistance only in preparation for

leaving the rolls. Of all cases closed in 1969, the reason
for termination in 13.6 percent was "employment or increased
earnings of the mother."[6] More detailed studies have indicated that an even larger proportion of AFDC women combine
work and welfare. For example, Burgess and Price showed
that even during the receipt of AFDC, 30 percent of the
women were working in some capacity.[7]

As shown in Chapter 2, the feature that characterizes a
great deal of work both on and off welfare is irregularity.
The Burgess and Price study showed a great preponderance of
both full- and part-time work done sporadically. Moreover,
the comparison of work effort before and during receipt of
AFDC reveals that work while receiving aid was more irregular than previous work. The Goodman study also indicated
that mothers used both employment and welfare as either concurrent or alternate methods of income maintenance.

Few inquiries have been made about whether past work
history in the AFDC population is a predictor of future work.
A study in Camden, New Jersey, in which the same women were
interviewed at two points in time, indicated that "past work
experience increases the likelihood that a welfare mother
will become a working mother."[8] This "persistence of labor
force status, a tendency for workers to remain workers and
non-workers to remain non-workers," was the strongest single
correlation among all variables predicting labor-force participation.[9]

In the Wisconsin study by Joel Handler and Ellen Jane
Hollingsworth, positive attitudes toward work were related
to past work. That is, those mothers who had worked recently tended to say that they would like to work, in contrast
with mothers who did not have a recent work history. However, the number of years they had worked in the past was
not related to current attitudes.[10] The Burgess and Price
study also showed continuing attachment to work. Of the respondents, 74 percent continued in the same employment
status. By and large, labor-force attachment persisted.[11]

In summary, it seems that most AFDC mothers do have
work experience either before, during, or after the receipt
of public assistance. The actual history of work is comprised of periods of employment and of less than full-time,
regular work. Public assistance appears to be used either
as a substitute for work or in conjunction with work. Although a work history in this low-income population may not
produce cumulative job skills and progressively higher earnings, it may still act as a determinant of future work as a
result of the apparent persistence of attachment to work.
Minimally, the presence of past work experience makes the
choice between work and welfare a more viable one.

Education and Skill

It has often been noted that formal education, translated into job skills that are further represented in occupational level, is a factor that influences labor-force attachment. Whether this is true in the case of AFDC recipients and how it is expressed in this context can be clarified by studying those women on AFDC who do work.

The 1967 AFDC study showed that working mothers were somewhat better educated than nonworking mothers, in that slightly fewer had less than 12 years of education and slightly more were high-school graduates. As indicated in Table 1, the mothers with more education tended to work full time, and the least educated (zero to eight years) tended to work part time.

TABLE 1

Percentage of AFDC Mothers Who Work, by Education, 1967

Years of Education	Percentage of Total Who Work		
	Total	Full Time	Part Time
0-8	15.0	6.0	9.0
9-11	15.2	7.9	7.3
12	19.8	11.0	8.8
13 plus	23.2	14.0	9.2

Source: The Family Assistance Act of 1970, U.S. Senate, Committee on Finance Hearings, Part 1 (Washington, D.C., 1970), p. 317.

The Goodman study also bears out the contention that women on AFDC are more likely to work and are likely to work more if they have had more education. The proportion of women who did not work during the 37-month period studied went down as educational achievement went up, although an important exception to this relationship was seen in those women who worked during the entire 37-month period. That the latter proportion did not vary with education gives further evidence of the "persistence of labor-force attachment." Education appears to have a positive effect on work effort, but how is it related to occupation? A 1967 characteristics survey shows that the "usual occupation" and the education of AFDC mothers are related positively until it comes

to domestic work. In this category, there are almost as
many high-school graduates as there are women with an educational level of less than nine years. Approximately 32.5
percent of high-school graduates have done domestic work,
and as many as 28 percent of those with some degree of college education list domestic work as their usual occupation.[13]

Educational level does not apparently have a direct bearing on occupation. Does occupation, however, act as a determinant of work effort? One would expect that the lower the
occupational level, the less likelihood of work; but data
from the characteristics study show this was not so. Mothers
who usually did private-household work were as likely to work
as those who sought professional work. Compared with the
total group of AFDC mothers, working AFDC mothers were more
likely to list domestic services as their usual occupation.
Private-household workers were also much more likely to work
part time than full time.[14] In effect, occupational level
did not seem to determine work effort among these women.

Although more-educated women are more likely to work,
more likely to work full time, and more likely to work more,
higher education does not necessarily determine the occupational bracket. As a group, working mothers had more education than AFDC mothers as a whole, but, nevertheless, they
were more likely to consider themselves domestic workers.
At the same time, the data show that fairly well-educated
women (high-school graduates and above) did a substantial
amount of domestic work and that being in domestic work made
work just as probable as being at the professional level.
The Camden study also bore this out. Among those respondents,
education and the amount of earnings were not related to each
other. The study concludes that "education influences the
decision to enter the working world but either does not encourage them (mothers) to work more regularly or does not
provide access to higher-paying jobs."[15]

This discontinuity in the relationships of education,
occupation, and work effort can be explained by the dichotomous nature of work on AFDC. The Burgess and Price study
considered race and residence in relation to employment.
The results reveal sharp differences between north and south,
urban and rural areas, and black and white AFDC mothers. The
southeast and southwest sections had the largest proportion
of AFDC cases in which the homemaker had no schooling. The
southeast had the lowest proportion of women who had gone beyond the eleventh grade.[16] The south also afforded the
greatest preponderance of mothers in domestic work, done
largely by black women.[17] Black women worked more in rural
than in urban areas. Conversely, the higher-skilled jobs,
held mostly by white women, were found in the north in large

metropolitan areas. The white women worked more in urban than in rural areas. A much larger proportion of black women worked during receipt of AFDC than did white women.[18]

There is some doubt whether educational achievement has the same effect on work patterns among Negroes as it does among whites. Podell's study found that the positive relationship between education and work history held for white but not for black women.[19] A recent study by Edward Opton, in California, found that education was relevant to "current employment status" and "total work time" measures, but that this educational advantage did not apply as much to black as to white welfare mothers.[20]

The linear association of education, occupation, and work effort is disturbed in the case of AFDC mothers by such factors as job discrimination, which nullifies the effects of education on occupation; cultural patterns that lead to the prevalence of certain occupations and that also focus on income accrual rather than on occupational mobility; a persistence of labor-force attachment as part of a female work ethic; and welfare policy that almost mandates work in certain southern rural areas where mainly agricultural work is available. These factors, in an AFDC population which was and has been over 45 percent black, may be more determinant of work and welfare patterns than education and skill.

This thesis about the twofold nature of work on AFDC might also help to explain the following paradox. In recent years, the educational and skill levels and the amount of earnings of AFDC mothers have risen. In 1967, only 15.9 percent of AFDC women had completed high school but had not gone further. By 1971 this figure was 19 percent.[21] In 1961, 7.7 percent of the mothers were designated as "skilled, blue-collar"; in 1968, 26 percent were so listed.[22] Average monthly earnings of the mother in AFDC families with income from work rose from $54.09 in 1961 to $221.25 in 1971.[23] Despite the growth in education, skill, and earnings, the proportion of AFDC mothers who combine work and welfare has remained the same: from 13 to 14 percent from 1961 to 1971.[24]

Although the proportion working has remained stable, there has been an increase in full-time work (from 4.6 percent in 1961 to 8.3 percent in 1971) and a corresponding decrease in part-time work.[25] This change can be explained by the increasing educational and skill levels of all AFDC mothers and of those who are at work.[26] As noted before, the more education, the more full-time work. The other half of the proposition, however--that the more educated women are more likely to work--has not increased the total proportion at work. The interpretation of this phenomenon may be found in the north-south dichotomy.

Table 2 was drawn up to examine the trends in work effort of AFDC mothers by region. From 1961 to 1971 the proportion of AFDC mothers in the middle Atlantic states who
were working increased, while the proportion in the southern
states decreased. In the north the proportion in full-time
work multiplied almost five times, whereas the proportion in
full-time work in the south increased only slightly. Conversely, the proportion in part-time work increased only
slightly in the north, but decreased radically in the south.
In effect, in the north there was an increase in the proportion of AFDC mothers working and working full time, while
there was a decrease in the proportion working in the south.

TABLE 2

Comparison of Working AFDC Mothers in Two Regions
(in percentages)

Region and Date	Total	Full-Time Work	Part-Time Work
Middle Atlantic			
1961	3.7	1.1	2.6
1967	6.9	3.8	3.1
1969	8.0	5.1	2.9
1971	8.5	5.4	3.1
South Atlantic			
1961	21.9	8.5	13.4
1967	20.6	9.6	11.0
1969	18.3	9.3	9.0
1971	18.8	10.4	8.4

Sources: Characteristics of Families Receiving Aid to
Families with Dependent Children, November-December 1961,
U.S. Department of Health, Education and Welfare (Washing-
ton, D.C., 1969), Table 23; Findings of the 1967 AFDC Study,
HEW (Washington, D.C., 1970), Table 38; Findings of the 1969
AFDC Study, HEW (Washington, D.C., 1970), Table 19; and
Findings of the 1971 AFDC Study, HEW (Washington, D.C.,
1972), Table 21.

Working AFDC mothers in northern states have more education, have more skills, and are more likely to work full time
and to have higher earnings. Although there are no data to
confirm it, more of them are probably white. This formulation

helps to explain the increase in full-time employment and
attests to the continuing dichotomous nature of work on AFDC.
While work effort in the northern states may have increased
merely by virtue of the fact that AFDC mothers have more education than formerly, it is not equally clear why southern
recipients have decreased their work effort. Such factors
as the responsiveness of southern welfare policy to the re-
verberations of the welfare-rights movement may have had a
negative effect on the work effort of southern AFDC mothers.
(An additional explanation can be found in Chapter 4 for why
part-time work has decreased.)

MONETARY DETERMINANTS

Decisions about income maintenance must essentially
emerge from three sources: the labor market, the welfare
system, and the individual's personal situation. Both wage
levels and welfare-benefit levels react with cultural and
labor-force variables to affect income-producing actions of
low-income people. Aspects of labor and welfare policy
other than the financial also serve to affect work and welfare decisions. This section deals only with the contribution of the welfare system to such decisions, as expressed
in welfare income.

Welfare Benefits

Welfare benefits have risen continuously in recent
years. The national average AFDC monthly payment per recipient increased from $27.45 in 1960 to $49.10 in June 1971,
or 78 percent. Using an "adjusted dollar amount" to reflect
real purchasing power results in an average monthly payment
in 1960 of $26.65, rising to $40.40 by 1971, a 51 percent
increase.[27]
Benefits have risen, not only absolutely, but in relation to income from work. A comparison of average earnings
of all private employees and the average monthly payment per
AFDC recipient from 1963 to 1971 shows that earnings increased by only 42 percent, while the AFDC payment increased
by 67 percent.[28] This national increase is reflected in New
York City, where Elizabeth Durbin compared welfare income
with wages. She discovered that during the 1960s "welfare
benefits increased more than average wages in manufacturing,
more than the minimum wage and more than the average or maximum unemployment compensation benefits." The welfare allowance by 1967 had risen 40 percent above its 1962 level, while

average wages had risen only 13 percent and minimum wages, 30 percent. Durbin also noted the many benefits-in-kind, such as medical services, which must be added to the grant to determine "real" welfare income.[29]

A further refinement of the comparison is contained in a Department of Labor study showing that earnings in the occupational groups in which AFDC mothers are distributed had risen only 4 percent a year between 1959 and 1967, while between 1961 and 1967 the average AFDC payment per family rose 5.5 percent a year. It concludes that "the markedly lower growth rates in earnings and income suggest that it would be even more difficult now than in the earlier period for welfare recipients to earn as much as they could receive from all sources while on welfare."[30]

Given the rise in welfare benefits, both absolutely and in relation to earnings, it is not surprising that the number of AFDC recipients has risen so dramatically. During the period 1965-70, expenditures for AFDC payments in all states combined went up 156.4 percent. Higher average payments accounted for 52 percent of this rise, and increase in recipients for 48 percent. When asked to give their interpretation of the increase in recipients for 1969-70 (22.4 percent in total), 17 states gave "higher assistance standards" as a reason.[31]

Although there is consensus that higher benefits produce more recipients, there appears to be some disagreement about the nature of this process. Two possible interpretations can be elicited from the literature. One is the "pool of eligibles" interpretation, which notes that, when grant levels become higher, more people become technically eligible for welfare since they have less income than the welfare payment. The other might be called the "desirability" interpretation, which says that higher grant levels make welfare more desirable as contrasted with other types of income, notably income from work.

David Gordon, who favors the "pool of eligibles" interpretation, explains the effect of higher benefits in New York City. In view of the income distribution, with large groups of people in dense low-income categories, even a slight rise in the benefit results in the creation of a very large number of new eligibles.[32] Durbin also attributes at least part of the rise in recipients to the higher benefits. However, she also considers "desirability" as a determinant and cites "improvements in the real value of welfare income relative to labor market earnings" as a factor in the increase.[33] In another study of the rise in welfare in New York City, William A. Johnson concludes that "more applicants are attracted by welfare assistance the more remunerative this assistance is; it supports, in other words, the assertion that welfare applicant behavior is economically rational."[34]

A study jointly conducted by the Department of Health, Education and Welfare and the New York State Department of Social Services compared wage levels, welfare-grant levels, and the extent of the use of AFDC in large cities. Wages were defined as the "average best wages" that an AFDC woman could make, and the "AFDC poor rate" was a measure of the number of AFDC cases per thousand persons in a city. The study was summarized as follows: "The relation between the difference in the average best wages and grant level and the AFDC poor rate proved to be statistically significant. As AFDC grants approached what the woman could actually receive in the labor market, more and more of them tend to choose AFDC." The size of the grant in relation to wages was related to the number of recipients in each city.[35]

Exactly how higher benefits are converted to more welfare recipients is not made explicit in either interpretation, but, in fact, each implies a very different process. In the "pool of eligibles" concept, the assumption is that certain people have certain incomes (probably from work) that fall somewhat above the welfare-benefit level, and they are therefore not eligible for welfare until the welfare benefit becomes higher than work income. At that point, they are eligible and may decide to apply for welfare. The determining factor is that the welfare benefit has now reached a level higher than their income. Gordon comments as follows:

> During the recent years in which grants were raised to those levels, thousands of poor families in New York City suddenly became "eligible" for welfare in the simple sense that their total disposable incomes now fell below what they were eligible to receive through welfare benefits or supplementary grants. Many of these families naturally decided to claim what the state had to offer.[36]

This formulation contains the notion that applicants are applying, not for the full welfare benefit, but for a partial benefit supplementary to their income from work. This, in effect, means that they will retain their previous work behavior while on assistance. Gordon elaborates: "Once that decision was made, a choice of welfare options—whether the husband should desert and the wife should apply

42

for AFDC or the husband should remain and the entire family apply for Home Relief—was relatively secondary."[37] The two options under the "pool of eligibles" theory are (a) the woman will go on AFDC, continue to work, and receive supplementary assistance; or (b) both mother and father will go on General Assistance (Home Relief), the father will continue to work, and the family will receive supplementary assistance.

In the "desirability" theory, which pits the welfare benefit against income from work, the implication is that, when the welfare grant reaches a certain level, a rational decision is made that income from work is not worth the effort. Prospective applicants, therefore, change their previous work behavior. They cease work or, if not working, refrain from finding work. In this case, there are three different options: (a) the woman in the female-headed family will stop work, go on AFDC, and receive a full grant; (b) in the intact family either the father or the mother or both will cease work and go on General Assistance for a full grant; and (c) there will be a "fiscal abandonment" or pretended desertion; that is, the woman (if she had worked before) will stop working and receive a full grant in AFDC, and the man will continue to work and contribute his income, which will not be budgeted.

Whether the effect of higher benefits is that people seek supplementary assistance while continuing to work or that they stop work and seek full assistance is salient to this discussion. Some insight into this issue may be obtained from data on nonassistance income and income from mothers' employment, shown in Table 3. If the "pool of eligibles" interpretation is adequate, this percentage of families having other income, including income from mothers' employment, should have increased as the number of recipient families increased. The figures in Table 3 show no sizable increases in either category, nationally or in New York City. There was a slight increase in the proportion of families with income from mothers' employment. The proportion of women who worked while on welfare also remained the same, although there was a small change in the direction of full-time work,[38] but not enough to explain the increase in recipients.

The case for supplementation and the retention of work behavior appears questionable under these circumstances. A more conclusive determination could be made if data were available on the specifics of work behavior of new recipients both before and during receipt of AFDC. Without such data, one can draw no substantive conclusion except to point out the need for such documentation and its importance in ascertaining the effect of welfare policy (in this case, benefit levels) on decisions about the use of work and welfare.

TABLE 3

Comparison of AFDC Families with Nonassistance Income
and Income from Mother's Employment, for the
United States and New York City
(in percentages)

	1961	1967	1969	1971
United States				
Families with nonassistance income	44.8	45.2	44.0	40.5
Families with income from mother's employment	12.5	13.4	13.7	13.7
New York City				
Families with nonassistance income	44.5	33.9	n.a.	n.a.
Families with income from mother's employment	2.3	4.4	6.5	n.a.

n.a. = not available

Sources: Characteristics of Families Receiving Aid to
Families with Dependent Children, November-December 1961,
U.S. Department of Health, Education and Welfare (Washington,
D.C., 1969), Table 49; Findings of the 1967 AFDC Study, HEW
(Washington, D.C., 1970), Table 115; Findings of the 1969
AFDC Study, HEW (Washington, D.C., 1970), Table 74; Findings
of the 1971 AFDC Study, HEW (Washington, D.C., 1972), Table
69; Report of Findings of Special Review of Aid to Families
with Dependent Children in New York City, HEW and New York
State Department of Social Services (Washington, D.C., 1969),
p. 70, Table 12; and Elizabeth F. Durbin, Welfare Income and
Employment (New York: Praeger, 1969), p. 84.

Income Disregards

It is customary to think that before the 1967 amendments, which called for disregarding a certain proportion of
the AFDC mother's employment income in computing the welfare
payment, there was a 100 percent "tax" on earnings, that is,
that every dollar earned was automatically deducted from the
assistance check. In fact, "work-related" expenses have
been disregarded in varying degrees by most states. In general, these expenses consist of deductions from the salary
check and additional personal needs connected with working.

In many states, work expenses added up to a substantial
amount of money. In Wisconsin, before the 1967 amendments,

an automatic $40 per month was exempted for work expenses, and additional expenses could be deducted as needed. Handler and Hollingsworth describe a "typical expense allowance" for a month in one county as the automatic $40 work expense, $64 for child care, $10 for transportation, and $2 for miscellaneous items, or $116 in all.[39] In New York City, work expenses included carfare, lunches, extra allowances for food, clothing, and personal care, union dues, taxes, and social security. Durbin cites an estimated average of $80 per month and notes that the real value of the assistance income must have included these allowances.[40]

Work-related expenses were not the only form of disregarded income before 1967. In many states in which the AFDC grants covered only a percentage of need, any earned income less than the difference between the amount of the payment and the standard of need was disregarded. Leonard Hausman says that "a substantial minority" of clients lived in such states.[41] Genevieve Carter wrote in 1968 that there were 20 such states, representing 25 percent of the national AFDC caseload. She correlated this information with the proportion of mothers working in each state in 1961 and concluded that "more AFDC mothers were employed in the States with employment incentives than in States that did not permit earnings to supplement the AFDC payment."[42]

A pertinent aspect of the use of these "disregards" is the extent to which people knew about them. Handler and Hollingsworth found that only 31 percent of the recipients in their sample knew about Wisconsin's earned-income policy (mentioned above) and about actual dollar amounts that would be deducted, whereas 53 percent had the process correct but the wrong dollar amounts. Most significantly, knowledge of the policy was not associated with either being currently employed or seeking or wanting work.[43]

In contrast to the varying ways of treating earned income before the 1967 amendments, Congress at that time instituted a national across-the-board mandatory policy of disregarding the first $30 and one-third of the remaining monthly employment income. This rule was, in fact, established to act as a work incentive for AFDC mothers in response to the alleged disincentive effects of the previous imputed 100 percent tax on earnings.

Just as in the case of work expenses, the degree of knowledge about the current policy is significant. In a recent study, Andrew Solarz concluded that "most respondents were unaware of even the most general meaning of the provision some six months after it went into effect."[44] Similarly, Edward Opton reported as follows:

> Most AFDC mothers do not know with any degree of clarity how much of any earnings

they would be allowed to keep, and how much
would be deducted from their welfare grants.
The complexity of the computations required
by welfare regulations makes it impossible,
for all practical purposes, for anyone but
a professional caseworker to estimate the
financial consequences of taking a job.[45]

Since this phase of the 1967 amendments went into effect nationally only in July 1969, there are no significant
data to answer fully the obvious question of whether the
disregard did, in fact, act as a work incentive: Did more
AFDC women work and did those who worked work more than before?* The Ninety-first Congress asked the same questions,
and the information forthcoming was tentative and incomplete.
On the basis of eleven months of experience, Illinois reported that (a) there was an increase in the number of cases
with budgeted employment income (some was attributed to increase in the total caseload and some to cases continued
that would have been closed by having reached the break-even
point under the earlier policy); (b) there was a decrease in
the amount of employment income budgeted (that is, more income was now disregarded); and (c) the number of cases closed
because of employment or increased earnings decreased.[46]
Another piece of evidence presented to Congress was that
from 1967 to 1969 the proportion of employed recipients rose
in the four states studied: Illinois, Ohio, Pennsylvania,
and New York; but only two of these states, Illinois and
Ohio, had the disregard in effect in 1969. The conclusion
was that "factors other than the earnings disregard brought
about the increase in the other two states and may have been
operative also in the two states that had the earnings disregard."[47]
Nationally, only 13.9 percent of mothers were at work
in 1971 while in receipt of AFDC, a proportion very close to
the 1969 figure. The proportion working full time, however,
had increased slightly, from 7.5 percent to 8.3 percent.[48]
It is difficult to evaluate the significance of these data
because the time period was so short. The disregard became
mandatory in July 1969, and the findings of the survey were
based on AFDC status in January 1971. Other factors, such
as the high unemployment rate, may also affect the reliabil-
ity of the data. Finally, since these figures reflect the
situation at one point in time, it is not clear what factors
were most influential.

---

*The "thirty and one-third" disregard is more fully ex-
amined in Chapter 4.

From the tentativeness of the above data, it is not possible really to know whether the 1969 disregard has, in fact, increased work effort. Even if it has, it does not appear that it would result in a "work only" decision. The Illinois experience, mentioned above, brings to light almost all the problems inherent in the disregard provision. Even in 1965, without the new ruling, from two-third to one-half of AFDC recipients could not earn enough to match the welfare payment.[49] The disregard pushes that payment up to a level that would require even more earning power. A paper from the Illinois Department of Public Aid states that it is "unlikely that an AFDC case can be closed under any foreseeable elevation in the earning potential of AFDC recipients," and that Illinois cannot close an AFDC case of a four-person family until the earnings reach $9,500 a year.[50] A study of the potential effects of the disregard in Michigan concludes that "it is unlikely that many AFDC recipients will be able to obtain jobs with earnings high enough to remove them from AFDC eligibility." In addition, the report continues:

> There is a strong incentive for the AFDC
> mother not to earn an income high enough,
> even if she could, to reach the zero grant
> point. This results from the fact that cer-
> tain additional services provided by the
> AFDC program are lost once the client leaves
> the program. The major services are child
> care and medical services.[51]

All this veers toward the prediction that, instead of leading to self-support and the option of work only, the disregard, if effective, will lead to some combination of work and welfare, thereby keeping people on AFDC. Indeed, the data given to Congress by Illinois, as tentative as they are on other points, affirmatively state that "there was no question . . . that the increase (of families with earnings) was due in part to the retention of greater numbers of families in the program than in the past as a direct result of the new policy."[52] When asked to account for the rise in AFDC cases from June 1969 to June 1970, 19 states gave the earnings disregard as the reason.[53]

The earnings disregard not only affects work and welfare decisions, it also impinges upon those who are at work only. Just as it creates incentives for working AFDC recipients to remain on AFDC, it also makes AFDC both available and attractive to working nonrecipient female heads of households. The Michigan study points out that the monthly financial incentive to enter or stay on AFDC comes to $312 for a one-child family earning $100 per month and to as much as

$461 for a three-child family earning $300 per month.[54]   Information presented to the Senate Finance Committee during
discussions of the Family Assistance Act compares the net
disposable incomes of four-person welfare and nonwelfare families earning the same amount in several states. In New
York, for example, a family earning $383 while on welfare
will end up with $461 monthly total income, whereas a non-
welfare family with the same earnings will net only $313.[55]

This inequity is further compounded by the policy of
eligibility for AFDC for families not on welfare. Unless a
family has been receiving AFDC within four months before application, it must be eligible without the application of
the disregard; that is, its income must fall below the grant,
not considering the disregard. In short, the disregard rule
cannot be a test of eligibility for those outside the system,
but it operates to afford a bonus to those within it. The
Michigan study sees this policy as "obviously an attempt to
prevent entry into the program," which could be viewed as
"discriminating heavily against the non-AFDC working poor."[56]

Inequity aside, the potential effect of such a provision
on the work-welfare decision is clear. A woman who is working and who wants to increase her income by obtaining welfare
benefits will have to stop work temporarily or work much less
in order to become eligible. The net effect of the earnings
disregard, then, is that, although it may encourage those on
welfare to work, it might be equally influential in encouraging those not on welfare to stop work and avail themselves of
welfare.

While the earnings disregard may have an effect on the
decision to work and/or use welfare, there is still another
type of disregard that can affect the pattern of work and welfare. This disregard concerns income earned on an irregular
or sporadic basis, income that cannot be depended upon for
continued and total support of the family but that, nevertheless, increases total income. Michael Piore says of this
supplementary income that, although it "may enable some families to live well above the welfare standard, the welfare
payment is probably essential to the families' survival."[57]

This kind of income can be disregarded in three different ways. It may be either not budgeted, not reported by the
caseworker, or not reported by the client. Some states take
the first option: they legitimate a route by which such income can be declared yet not budgeted. In Massachusetts it
is called "casual income" and defined as any amount that is
"not received periodically or continuously" and that "cannot
be computed or predicted over a period of time." In Wisconsin, this is called "inconsequential income." This kind of
disregard may encourage the client to choose sporadic and

irregular work rather than regular work. In states in which there is no such disregard, the "thirty and one-third" earnings disregard may fulfill the function of encouraging this kind of work pattern, since the proportion of earnings taken into account in budgeting goes up past the $30 point.

When supplementary income is not legitimated, it still may be disregarded by the caseworker. Handler and Hollingsworth found that in Wisconsin many working mothers "kept a good deal of their earnings," that the earned-income policy was not being uniformly enforced, and that caseworkers tended to exercise their discretion and treated a great deal of earned income as "inconsequential," whether or not it technically fell into that category. Handler and Hollingsworth further speculated that "because of lack of enforcement, the earned-income policy does not have a disincentive effect."[58]

The third route for disregarding supplementary or irregular income is failure of the client to report it. The kind of work done to earn irregular and sporadic income is equally irregular and sporadic and lends itself to a "flexibility of disclosure" that is consistent with not reporting.[59] In addition, the welfare machinery for budgeting such income (a system geared to regular budget deductions) would leave the client's grant continuously confused and in a state of arrears if this type of income were conscientiously reported. This is probably why some states have instituted a legitimate route for not budgeting such income.

There appears to be some evidence that unreported irregular income is disregarded. In New York City, where no such disregard exists officially, earned income, whether known to the caseworker or not, is in some part disregarded. One study showed that 3 percent of the cases studied were ineligible because the families had income in excess of need, and that over two-thirds of these had this excess because of earnings.[60] The possibility of earning small or irregular income that is not budgeted and is therefore an addition to the welfare grant may act as an incentive for women already on AFDC to remain there and to reject regular employment either alone or as budgeted into the welfare grant.

It is clear that all the earned-income disregards, taken together, add up to a substantial amount and affect the work-welfare decision. As discussed above, they should tend to encourage the combination work-welfare choice and discourage the choices that involve work only or welfare only. The disregards also have an influence on the work or welfare patterns that emerge. The national figures on work in AFDC may have increased in the direction of full-time employment as a result of the "thirty and one-third" rule, which permits supplementation of the higher salaries earned by full-time work. On the other hand, the disregards may also make part-time and sporadic work more feasible, since work that was previously unreported may now be declared and disregarded under the "thirty and one-third" provision.

CULTURAL DETERMINANTS

Even when the impact of the above structural determinants on the work-welfare choice is considered, there still remains a residual area of influence not accounted for by such concrete considerations as welfare benefits and occupational levels. This area represents or reflects the lifestyle or culture of one group of people for whom this choice is necessary and feasible. No doubt the AFDC population contains many types of families, but a predominant, seemingly large sector within it can be singled out as forming a "cultural" unit having a specific way of life.* This group has been delineated as the "female-based" household, in which "serial monogamy" is the mating pattern.[62] Walter B. Miller describes the group as "hard-core" and the cultural system as "lower-class." Miller estimated the size of this group in the United States population to be about 25 million in 1958, and he saw it as increasing.

Although the principal indicator of any cultural unit is lifestyle, a concept which does not easily lend itself to quantification, some other measures such as the prevalence of female-headed families and births out of wedlock, can be

---

*In this section, I will deal only with the proponents of the cultural point of view who, in essence, posit a "culture of poverty." In very basic terms and in the words of Oscar Lewis, its originator, a culture of poverty is "a design for living within the constraints of poverty, passed on from generation to generation, thereby achieving stability and persistence."[61] Without delving into the fine points of cultural theory, it can be stipulated that a culture contains at least the following basic dimensions: (a) a consistent core of average behavior (what most people do), (b) a socializing capacity, (c) a normative function (what is good and bad), (d) a certain relationship between behavior and values, and (e) some resistance to change. These five dimensions or attributes of culture can be posed against the "constraints of poverty" and what all "culture-of-poverty" adherents agree is basic: that a major factor in shaping the other elements of its culture is the economic situation of the family.

used to define the significance and size of the "hard-core" sector of American society here being discussed. In the United States in 1960, 9.9 percent of all familes were female-headed; 8.7 percent of the white and 22.4 percent of nonwhite families were in this category. In 1968, 10.6 percent of all families were female-headed, and 8.9 percent of whites and 26.4 percent of nonwhites were so designated.[63] The illegitimate birthrate went from 5.3 percent in 1960 to 6.8 percent in 1964 to 9.0 percent in 1967.[64] This group, if these "hard measures" are to be taken as indicators, is indeed sizable and also increasing.

Within AFDC, national statistics show that families in which the father is not married to the mother increased from 21.3 percent in 1961 to 27.7 percent in 1971, and families broken by divorce, separation, or desertion increased from 40.5 percent in 1961 to 43.5 percent in 1971.[65] In addition, 43.5 percent of all AFDC families in 1971 had at least one illegitimate child, and 25.3 percent were families in which there was one mother of all the children but two or more different fathers.[66]

If we are to characterize this group as having a "distinctive cultural system,"[67] it is clear that there is such a group both in the population at large and in AFDC, a group of no small proportions whose size appears to be expanding. The AFDC program reflects the large lower-class group and also draws upon it for a significant part of its clientele. The question of whether the program itself aids in sustaining such a group has been raised by some observers.

In order to evaluate the features of this lifestyle that are relevant to the work and welfare decisions at issue here, it would be fruitful to locate those elements within this culture that are consistent with such choices. The social sciences have contributed descriptions of the lower class, but there is little focus on the use of welfare and on work for women in this context. It is necessary, therefore, to explore more general characteristics that can be associated with the use of work and welfare. This is not to say that they are not pertinent but that the link to work and welfare has not been forged by observers who are interested primarily in culture. Three strands of behavior described in the literature seem to be meaningful--the male-female conflict, the transmission of a welfare culture, and the meaning of income.

The Male-Female Conflict

The "serial monogamy" mating pattern and the female-based household are the result of a family structure that consists of legal marriages that dissolve and nonlegal unions that occur alone or are interspersed with marriages. In both cases, welfare provides a choice. It permits the man to leave the family unit by providing an economic alternative to his being there. In 1965, Daniel Patrick Moynihan pointed to the "pathological" nature of black family structure as the root cause of welfare dependency. The failure of the male to assume the usual functions of support and the reversal of roles between men and women lay behind a way of life that depended heavily on welfare.[68] It was the man's inability or unwillingness to be the breadwinner that caused the need for the family to use AFDC.

Two years earlier, on the basis of a small empirical study, Jane Kronick had concluded that women on AFDC were on welfare because they had failed in their basic relationships, especially the marital relationship. She cited their "difficulty encountered in human relationships which is not unrelated to their difficulties in financial management" and the "social and psychological pathology which is impinging upon the relationships that the ADC woman established with other individuals."[69] To both Moynihan and Kronick, it appears that the family has somehow failed as a unit, and AFDC is utilized to compensate for this failure.

Later proponents of a less evaluative concept of the culture of poverty, such as Lee Rainwater and Ulf Hannerz, explain the breakup of the lower-class family as a result of a great deal of marital discord and a virtual "battle of the sexes." Hannerz poses two models of behavior in the ghetto: the "mainstream" model, which is closely allied to the dominant culture of society, and the "ghetto-specific" model, which is the poverty subculture in operation. He explains the failure of the marriage in this way:

> The conflict element in the male-female union
> is probably particularly dependent on the
> fact that unions of ghetto-specific forms are
> continuously compared, if only implicitly, to
> the mainstream model of marriage for which
> the ghetto-specific ascribed resources are a
> poor basis.[70]

The lower-class wife makes demands upon the husband that, due to the economic circumstances in which he finds himself, he cannot fulfill. Elliot Liebow describes ghetto men as follows: "Convinced of their inadequacies, not only do they not seek out those few better-paying jobs which test their resources, but they actively avoid them, gravitating in a mass to the menial, routine jobs which offer no challenge--

and therefore pose no threat--to the already diminished images they have of themselves."[71] The marriage founders on two counts: "The economic marginality of husbands seemed generally to be converted into a moral issue; the wives maintain not that their husbands cannot but that they will not support them."[72] In addition, the husband begins to partake of the "street life"--gambling, drinking, and seeking out other women as sexual partners. The wife asks the husband to leave. Rainwater found that 60 percent of his sample had marriages broken by divorce or separation (of these, 40 percent for sexual infidelity), and, in 27 percent of these cases, the husband would not support the family or would not work.[73] However, separation appeared not to have the onerous implications that it has for other women. Rainwater explains further:

> Part of the woman's passivity has to do with her perception of the husband as not particularly valuable even if he were to end his disloyal activities. She does not perceive herself to be as dependent on her husband as does the white lower-class wife. She does not generally regard her husband as a good provider and she knows that she can probably scrape by with work or with family and welfare support even if the marriage is terminated.
>   For the woman, taken-for-grantedness involves most centrally the knowledge that she can head a household if she must, that this is not a remarkable event in her world, and that her culture provides techniques and support for doing this.[74]

This model of self-sufficiency--of being able to do without the husband--is buttressed by the availability of welfare, which acts not only as a source of economic sustenance but also as a paternal or caretaking institution substituting for the missing male. Sydney Bernard's 1964 study of AFDC women quotes them as saying that "Mother's Aid is a better husband, anyway, because you can count on it."[75] Kronick, too, sees welfare as filling the gap that a woman's inadequacy in relationships has created. Certainly, welfare is a more secure source of income than the "errant" husband could have provided.

After the woman is separated from her husband for some time, a common pattern is to take on a "boyfriend," and, in time, perhaps, several more. The woman may now begin to

look like her male counterpart. It should be remembered,
however, that for her a close and permanent relationship
with a husband has failed. She then contents herself with
relationships that contain less commitment, with "extra-
residential unions, often of short duration." Rainwater
wrote: "The extent may vary to which the boyfriend contrib-
utes to or takes from the material assets of the family. In
some cases the man may make direct and regular money contributions, and in other cases he makes regular purchases of
particular goods."[76]

Bernard found that one-third of his respondents received
financial help from boyfriends. In addition to providing financial help, the boyfriend provides an emotionally "safe"
relationship: "For her part, the woman is not forced to set
standards for his behavior that he obviously will not be
able to meet, and in many cases she is able to preserve welfare support, a stable if small income that would have to be
foregone if the relationship were legitimated."[77] This is
not to imply that the boyfriend does not become the father
of another child, which he may or may not support or which
he may support sporadically. He may, in fact, not even acknowledge the child to be his. The boyfriend, then, appears
to afford the dual financial asset of providing some measure
of support additional to work or welfare income without in-
terfering with eligibility for AFDC.

The particular variety of male-female relationship described here is peculiar to the lower class that makes up a
large part of the population-at-risk in AFDC. The conflict
and subsequent breakup of the marriage (or nonlegal union)
and the availability of welfare appear to reinforce each
other in the process that produces decisions to use welfare,
although the causal sequence between the variables is not
clear. If, as Rainwater says, the woman does not depend on
the man because she knows that she can manage with either
work or welfare, the breakup of the marriage or other such
relationship may, in fact, lead to either route--work or
welfare. Welfare, however, is not available while the male
is present; work is. However, in both cases, it is the loss
of the male breadwinner that makes such a choice necessary.

The Culture Around and Above: Welfare

Many observers of lower-class life have noted the in-
tensity of interaction in a lower-class neighborhood.
Kronick's study found this high degree of social intercourse
in two-thirds of her sample. Troubles are shared, help is
given, knowledge is transmitted. Knowledge about welfare

permeates this kind of community. Kronick wrote that "information regarding public assistance is so pervasive in this population that a single [referral] service cannot be isolated."[78] The availability of AFDC as a resource is known, not only because of high interaction and communication, but also because of high use. In describing a ghetto community, Charles Valentine said: "Every [welfare] check day truly galvanizes Blackston, first with expectation, then with delayed commercial and credit transactions, and finally with celebrations." He went on to say: "If those who benefit indirectly are included, there can be little doubt that a majority of our Afro-American population and perhaps of the whole community gain some portion of their livelihood from the welfare system."[79] Welfare is not only known and used but also accepted. Louis Kriesberg found that only 5 percent of all the mothers he studied (including nonwelfare mothers) said they would think worse of mothers for going on welfare.[80] Bernard, too, found welfare an acceptable alternative among his respondents.

In addition to the culture "around," which harbors a great deal of knowledge and use of welfare, there is also the culture "above," which is expressed in the concept of intergenerational dependency on welfare. Both the horizontal and the vertical elements of culture are pertinent to the transmission of a "welfare culture." In this respect, Hannerz, paraphrasing Oscar Lewis, says that "slum children soon absorb the values and attitudes of their subculture so that they may not be able later to take advantage of increased opportunities," and "once the culture of poverty comes into existence, it tends to perpetuate itself in new generations."[81]

Indeed, to the extent that people currently on welfare have parents who have been on welfare and children who are on welfare, this proposition can be documented. In a Greenleigh study in 1964, over 43 percent of families then on AFDC had parents who had been dependent at some time.[82] In Podell's study of New York City, only 15 percent of the mothers on welfare reported that their parents had been assisted at some time,[83] but the Burgess and Price national study of 1960 reported that 40 percent of adults in their ADC sample "had been reared in homes in which some form of public aid had been received at some time."[84] Podell's study also indicated that about one-fourth of the mothers on welfare had at least one sibling on welfare at the time of the study.[85]

From these accounts it seems that welfare is both familiar and acceptable in many lower-class communities. The alleged stigma that supposedly acts as a deterrent to the use

of welfare in some other types of areas may not be a pertinent factor here. There is a difference between stigma from
the overall community and stigma from one's own community,
particularly if it is a ghetto community. Although stigma
may flow from the outside community to the welfare recipient,
the effect may be nullified by the lack of stigma in the im-
mediate environment.

The extent to which work for women is a community norm,
in the same way that welfare appears to be in ghetto areas,
is not clear. Goodman attempted to correlate the welfare
stigma with employment on the notion that AFDC recipients
may not work because welfare is an acceptable alternative
(not stigmatizing) or that they do work because welfare is
stigmatizing. He reported as follows:

> The amount of employment is not positively
> correlated with the feeling that receiving
> welfare is socially stigmatizing. On the
> contrary, respondents with the longest rec-
> ords of employment are less likely to feel
> that welfare status is scorned than those
> who worked less of the time or not at all.[86]

Although work effort among AFDC and potential AFDC recipients appears not to be affected by the acceptability of welfare, such acceptability should have a significant impact on
the use of welfare.

The Meaning of Income

Since the work-welfare choice involves alternative ways
of obtaining income, the meaning of income in lower-class
culture should in some way be related to the choice. Whereas the working middle-class person usually derives his income from one contractual source--a job or business--the
upper-class person probably has several sources, such as job
or business, stock market, inheritances, annuities, rents,
etc. This relationship to income may be seen as enterprising rather than contractual. It is a form of income accrual.
The lower-class person also has an enterprising, acquisitive
attitude toward income, and income in the lower class is
also accrued.

Valentine characterizes this relationship as follows:
"A great many individuals manage to garner small increments
of income from several or numerous different origins." He
found that basic income sources, such as employment, were
most commonly supplemented by "partial, supplementary welfare

payments, gambling, gifts and loans from kinsmen and other network associates, miscellaneous neighborhood service and odd jobs."[87] Bernard's "high users" of welfare live a life of "creative instability." They must tap many sources and be willing to shift gears or move. These high users were willing to tolerate instability of income sources in order to receive the greatest return from a variety of sources. In commenting on the unstable and unclear nature of the structure of income, Valentine wrote:

> We have found that the detailed phenomena of income and occupation are quite complex and frequently obscure. It appears that under fluctuating and marginal economic conditions, the actual sources of general subsistence and occasional surplus become multiple, varied, and rapidly shifting.[88]

Income, then, tends to be procured in small amounts from several sources, which are inclined to change.

Another dimension of income acquisition is its exploitative nature. Bernard describes "an inventive and exploratory attitude toward income sources based on how much they yield rather than on their moral or legal status."[89] Kronick discusses the financial management of her respondents as "techniques designed to protect their security of residence and to maximize their material possessions."[90] Rainwater adds:

> Exploitative relations with others are the dynamic aspect of the basic distrust pervasive within the ghetto community. . . . When opportunities for exploiting others are not available or are considered too dangerous, the individual resigns himself to what comes his way and is preoccupied with the mechanics of getting the little bit for which he has a chance--an ADC check or a low-wage job.[91]

Bernard says of his respondents on welfare: "Some . . . were careful to comply with regulations, but others learned the system and used it to their own best advantage."[92] Valentine also comments on the use of welfare in his ghetto neighborhood:

> A great many poor people put much energy and ingenuity into getting all they can from this apparatus (the welfare system). . . . Most welfare recipients supplement their income

from any of a wide variety of sources, many
of which are technically illicit in terms
of the official rules of the system.[93]

Michael Schwartz and George Henderson wrote of the people on
or likely to be on welfare: "The adaptations over generations have in many cases become 'functionally autonomous.'
They are, for many, now a preferred way of life; an appropriate life style that includes 'bunking in,' welfare chis-
eling, etc."[94]

These acquisitive, exploitative features of income retrieval that tend to characterize this hard-core group give
rise to corollary attitudes toward work and welfare. In
this kind of framework, work-welfare options may not be
dichotomous or mutually exclusive. If the pattern is to ac-
crue as much income as possible from several sources, work-
welfare choices may supplement rather than substitute for
each other, and both may become part of a larger income-
maintenance picture, which includes still other alternatives.
The options also may shift and be used serially, alone, or
in conjunction with other income sources at different times
in an individual's life.

Depending upon welfare-administrative feasibility, members of this group could both work and receive assistance,
either legitimately or illegitimately, in an attempt to maximize total income. The risks to be taken in the latter
course of action would be tolerated in return for a larger
total income. In this kind of situation, regular and continuous work might be shunned as not compatible with a pattern of variable income accrual, and work that lends itself
to the pattern might be utilized accordingly.

CONCLUSIONS

Although the perspectives reviewed here may be valid in
their description of the variables that impinge on the AFDC
and potential AFDC population, they are only partial expla-
nations of the choices regarding work-welfare options. They
are single, discrete influences that can be abstracted for
analytic purposes, but they do not in reality have the kind
of direct, distinct effect that the logic of the analysis
seems to indicate. Even if all possible factors were considered at the same time in some kind of serial or weighted
progression, it would not be clear how they combined and
interacted in a single individual to effect a relevant decision. That could be clarified only by a study of the individual. What can be attempted here are some broad tentative

outlines that relate the pieces to each other in a coherent fashion.

It can be accepted as given that a large part of the adult AFDC population consists of low-skilled, low-paid female workers or potential workers who are tied to a marginal, fluctuating job market and who have the care of children as a primary function. When women in these circumstances experience the loss of a male breadwinner, when welfare is available, and when the culture does not decry its use, then the choice to use welfare, either alone or in conjunction with work, seems natural. In those instances when they choose work, the work is characteristically irregular, and it may be supplemented by welfare or other sources, such as contributions from husband or boyfriend. When work is not available, pays too little, or is prevented by family obligations, welfare may become the only source of income for a period of time. Then work, either reported or unreported, may be started again or welfare may be supplemented by sources other than work.

In this view, work and welfare are not seen as mutually exclusive. Martin Rein has pointed out that the two systems mesh in complex ways. He writes: "Welfare is a form of social provision when income is absent, interrupted, or inadequate, and not simply a cash transfer system operating outside the world of work."[95] The sporadic nature of work fits in with the use of welfare on an intermittent basis, with one cycling into the other or supplementing the other. In this regard, the Burgess and Price study pointed out that irregular work increased after the receipt of AFDC, since such work was consistent with welfare status. The breakup of the marriage and the subsequent use of periodic, less committed relationships is also related to the availability and the intermittent use of welfare.

If welfare status is seen as consisting of "this complex of activities as a whole" (activities that include both work and welfare and other means of income maintenance), then work and welfare are not adequately conceptualized in terms of a dichotomous choice.

NOTES

1. Elaine M. Burgess and Daniel O. Price, An American Dependency Challenge (Chicago: American Public Welfare Association, 1963), p. 250.
2. Lawrence Podell, Families on Welfare in New York City (New York: City University of New York, 1967), p. 16.

3. Leonard H. Goodman, Welfare Policy and its Consequences for the Recipient Population, U.S. Department of Health, Education and Welfare (Washington, D.C., 1969), p. 113.

4. Preliminary Report of Findings of the 1969 AFDC Study, U.S. Department of Health, Education and Welfare (Washington, D.C., 1970), Table 38.

5. Characteristics of Families Receiving Aid to Families with Dependent Children, November-December 1961, U.S. Department of Health, Education and Welfare (Washington, D.C., 1963), Table 23; Findings of the 1967 AFDC Study, U.S. Department of Health, Education and Welfare (Washington, D.C., 1970), Table 38; Findings of the 1969 AFDC Study, U.S. Department of Health, Education and Welfare (Washington, D.C., 1970), Table 19.

6. Reasons for Opening and Closing Public Assistance Cases, U.S. Department of Health, Education and Welfare (Washington, D.C., 1969), Table 9.

7. Burgess and Price, op. cit.

8. Samuel Z. Klausner et al., "The Work Incentive Program: Making Adults Economically Independent" (Philadelphia: Center for the Study of the Acts of Man, 1972), p. 10 (mimeographed).

9. Ibid., p. 15.

10. Joel F. Handler and Ellen Jane Hollingsworth, "Work, Welfare, and the Nixon Reform Proposals," Stanford Law Review 22, no. 5 (May 1970): 918, 919.

11. Burgess and Price, op. cit., p. 29.

12. Goodman, op. cit., p. 120.

13. The Family Assistance Act of 1970, U.S. Senate, Committee on Finance, Hearings (Washington, D.C., 1970), p. 318.

14. Ibid., p. 317.

15. Klausner, op. cit., p. 22.

16. Burgess and Price, op. cit., p. 247.

17. Ibid., p. 248.

18. Ibid., p. 30.

19. Podell, op. cit., p. 85.

20. Edward M. Opton, Jr., Factors Associated with Employment among Welfare Mothers (Berkeley: Wright Institute, 1971), p. 66.

21. Findings of the 1967 AFDC Study, op. cit., Table 40; Findings of the 1971 AFDC Study, U.S. Department of Health, Education and Welfare (Washington, D.C., 1972), Table 23.

22. Perry Levinson, "How Employable are AFDC Women?" Welfare in Review 8, no. 4 (July-August 1970): 13.

23. Characteristics of Families Receiving AFDC, op. cit., Table 50; Findings of the 1971 AFDC Study, op. cit., Table 56.

24. Characteristics of Families Receiving AFDC, op. cit., Table 23; Findings of the 1967 AFDC Study, op. cit., Table 38; Findings of the 1969 AFDC Study, op. cit., Table 19; Findings of the 1971 AFDC Study, op. cit., Table 21.

25. Characteristics of Families Receiving AFDC, op. cit., Table 23; Findings of the 1971 AFDC Study, op. cit., Table 21.

26. National Cross-Tabulations from the 1967 and 1969 AFDC Studies, U.S. Department of Health, Education and Welfare (Washington, D.C., 1971), Table 28.

27. Trend Report: Graphic Presentation of Public Assistance and Related Data, 1971, U.S. Department of Health, Education and Welfare (Washington, D.C., 1972), p. 7.

28. Sar A. Levitan, Martin Rein, and David Marwick, Work and Welfare Go Together (Baltimore: Johns Hopkins University Press, 1972), p. 14.

29. Elizabeth F. Durbin, Welfare Income and Employment (New York: Praeger, 1969), pp. 6, 82.

30. The Potential for Work among Welfare Parents, U.S. Department of Labor (Washington, D.C., 1969), p. 8.

31. Trends in AFDC 1965-1970, U.S. Department of Health, Education and Welfare (Washington, D.C., n.d.), p. 6.

32. David M. Gordon, "Income and Welfare in New York City," Public Interest, No. 16 (Summer 1969), p. 81.

33. Durbin, op. cit., p. 143.

34. William A. Johnson, "The Welfare Crisis: The Growth of Dependency in New York City" (Draft, New York: Rand Institute, 1971), Appendix p. 12.

35. Report of Findings of Special Review of Aid to Families with Dependent Children in New York City, U.S. Department of Health, Education and Welfare and New York State Department of Social Services (Washington, D.C., 1969), p. 43.

36. Gordon, op. cit.

37. Ibid.

38. Characteristics of Families Receiving AFDC, op. cit., Table 23; Findings of the 1967 AFDC Study, op. cit., Table 38; Findings of the 1969 AFDC Study, op. cit., Table 19; Findings of the 1971 AFDC Study, op. cit., Table 21.

39. Handler and Hollingsworth, op. cit., p. 927.

40. Durbin, op. cit., p. 93.

41. Leonard J. Hausman, "Potential for Financial Self-Support among AFDC and AFDC-UP Recipients," Southern Economic Journal 36, no. 1 (July 1969): 60 n. 3.

42. Genevieve W. Carter, "The Employment Potential of AFDC Mothers," <u>Welfare in Review</u> 6, no. 4 (July-August 1968): 8.

43. Handler and Hollingsworth, op. cit., pp. 920-22.

44. Andrew K. Solarz, "Effects of the Earnings Exemption Provision on AFDC Recipients," <u>Welfare in Review</u> 9, no. 1 (January-February 1971): 19.

45. Opton, op. cit., p. 196.

46. <u>The Family Assistance Act of 1970</u>, pp. 1012-14.

47. Ibid., p. 1012.

48. <u>Findings of the 1971 AFDC Study</u>, op. cit., Table 21.

49. Hausman, op. cit., pp. 60-66.

50. "The Income Exemption in the AFDC Program: Problems Presented by Federal Law and Policy," Illinois Department of Public Aid (Draft, Springfield, Ill., 1969), p. 18.

51. <u>AFDC Employment Incentives</u>, Michigan Department of Social Services (Lansing, 1970), p. 7.

52. <u>Family Assistance Act of 1970</u>, pp. 1012, 1013.

53. <u>Trends in AFDC 1965-1970</u>, op. cit., p. 13.

54. <u>AFDC Employment Incentives</u>, op. cit., p. 10.

55. <u>Family Assistance Act of 1970</u>, op. cit., p. 201.

56. <u>AFDC Employment Incentives</u>, op. cit., p. 9.

57. Michael J. Piore, "Income Maintenance and Labor Market Entry: The FAP Proposal and the AFDC Experience," <u>Poverty and Human Resources Abstracts</u> 5, no. 3 (May-June 1970): 13.

58. Handler and Hollingsworth, op. cit., p. 922.

59. See Chapter 2.

60. <u>Report of Findings of Special Review of AFDC in N.Y.C.</u>, op. cit., p. 173.

61. Ulf Hannerz, <u>Soulside: Inquiries into Ghetto Culture and Community</u> (New York: Columbia University Press, 1969), p. 179.

62. Walter B. Miller, "Lower Class Culture as a Generating Milieu of Gang Delinquency," <u>Journal of Social Issues</u> 14, no. 3 (March 1958): 6.

63. <u>Statistical Abstract of the United States: 1969</u>, U.S. Bureau of the Census (Washington, D.C., 1969), p. 36.

64. Ibid., p. 50.

65. <u>Characteristics of Families Receiving AFDC</u>, op. cit., Table 12; <u>Findings of the 1971 AFDC Study</u>, op. cit., Table 15.

66. <u>Findings of the 1971 AFDC Study</u>, op. cit., Tables 32 and 31.

67. Miller, op. cit., p. 6.

68. Daniel Patrick Moynihan, <u>The Negro Family: The Case for National Action</u> (Washington, D.C.: Government Printing Office, 1965).

69. Jane C. Kronick, "Attitudes Toward Dependency: A Study of 119 AFDC Mothers" (Bryn Mawr, Pa.: Bryn Mawr College, 1963), p. 37 (mimeographed).

70. Hannerz, op. cit., p. 102.

71. Elliot Liebow, Tally's Corner (Boston: Little, Brown, 1967), p. 54.

72. Lee Rainwater, Behind Ghetto Walls (Chicago: Aldine, 1970), p. 174.

73. Ibid., p. 170.

74. Ibid., p. 165.

75. Sydney E. Bernard. "Economic and Social Adjustment of Low-Income Female-Headed Families" (unpublished Ph.D. thesis, Brandeis University, 1964), p. 57.

76. Rainwater, op. cit., p. 181.

77. Ibid., p. 187.

78. Kronick, op. cit., p. 44.

79. Charles A. Velentine, "Blackston: A Progress Report on a Community Study in Urban Afro-America," study sponsored by the National Institute of Mental Health, U.S. Department of Health, Education and Welfare (February 1970), p. 30 (mimeographed).

80. Louis Kriesberg, Mothers in Poverty--A Study of Fatherless Families (Chicago: Aldine, 1970), p. 149.

81. Hannerz, op. cit., p. 181.

82. Greenleigh Associates, Poverty-Prevention or Perpetuation (New York: Greenleigh Associates, 1964), p. 32.

83. Podell, op. cit., p. 28.

84. M. Elaine Burgess, "Poverty and Dependency: Some Selected Characteristics," Journal of Social Issues 21, no. 1 (January 1965): 93.

85. Podell, op. cit.

86. Goodman, op. cit., p. 136.

87. Valentine, op. cit., pp. 19, 21.

88. Ibid., p. 19.

89. Bernard, op. cit., p. 17.

90. Kronick, op. cit., p. 74.

91. Rainwater, op. cit., p. 74.

92. Bernard, op. cit., p. 65.

93. Valentine, op. cit., p. 30.

94. Michael Schwartz and George Henderson, "The Culture of Unemployment: Some Notes on Negro Children," in Blue-Collar World, edited by Arthur B. Shostak and William Gomberg (Englewood Cliffs, N.J.: Prentice-Hall, 1964), p. 464.

95. Martin Rein, Social Policy: Issues of Choice and Change (New York: Random House, 1970), p. 397.

4

WORK INCENTIVES:
"THIRTY AND ONE-THIRD"

In 1967, in an attempt to control the ever-growing AFDC rolls, Congress passed an amendment to Title IV of the Social Security Act that permitted AFDC adult recipients to keep a certain part of what they earned. This, coupled with other measures designed to propel AFDC parents into the labor market, was intended to act as a work incentive. It was a response to the assumption that before this time, earnings of working AFDC caretakers (mostly mothers) were reduced "dollar-for-dollar," a policy that appeared to have severe work disincentive effects.

The amendment stipulated that all states should disregard the first $30 per month plus one-third of remaining earned income in computing the AFDC monthly benefit. Work expenses were already being disregarded in compliance with a 1962 amendment, and child care expenses, too, were either to be supplied by the welfare agency or granted by that agency as a "service." The "thirty and one-third" was an additional disregard. However, this exemption was only available to families already on AFDC. A new family applying would have to be eligible without the application of the disregard. The purpose of the amendment was to encourage AFDC recipients to work, but not to encourage working non-recipients to enter the AFDC program. It was hoped that the disregard of earned income would result in a notable increase in the number of AFDC parents who would consequently make the effort to work and optimally become self-maintaining.

Inherent in the attempt to induce work through the disregard was the broader notion that work incentives and work behavior are causally connected. It is important, therefore, to determine whether, in fact, the disregard had the desired outcome--not only as a single event but as part of the larger context of welfare reform in which work incentives

are so important. In this chapter, we will attempt to find
out what effect the "thirty and one-third" disregard has had
on the work behavior of AFDC mothers, and what this means in
relation to other aspects of welfare policy. In order to
make an estimate of what actually happened in regard to this
earnings exemption we will look at (a) national data on the
AFDC program, (b) empirical studies that attempt to evaluate
the results of the disregard, and (c) "tax rates" and what
part they play.

THE NATIONAL DATA

The earnings exemption, though legislated in 1967, became mandatory in the states in July 1969; and the most recent Department of Health, Education and Welfare survey of
AFDC took place in January 1971. This short 18-month period
is not sufficient, of itself, to yield conclusive data on
the question of whether the earnings exemption had the intended effect of increasing work among AFDC mothers. Notwithstanding this limitation, the data can be used as part
of a more comprehensive analysis, and also to indicate
trends in significant areas.
There are at least three ways in which the national
data can be helpful: it can tell us whether more women were
at work after than were before the institution of the disregard, whether more cases were closed for employment, and
whether the earnings level of those at work had gone up.
These, in fact, are the three dimensions upon which the work
behavior of recipients can be measured. If the disregard
were successful, we would expect positive gains in all three
areas. We would predict that more mothers would be at work,
more cases would be closed as a result of work, and there
would be higher earnings.
We find that the proportion of mothers at work while on
AFDC has remained at about 13 percent of all AFDC mothers
since 1961. In 1969 there were 13.3 percent mothers working
and by 1971 this figure rose very slightly to 13.9 percent.[1]
The disregard period from 1969 to 1971 did not result in a
significantly larger proportion at work nationally. Our
second measure, cases closed for "employment or increased
earnings of the mother," _dropped_ from 13.6 percent in 1969 to
6.5 percent in 1972, a reduction of over 50 percent.[2] This
data shows that a much smaller proportion of AFDC cases were
closed for employment of the mother after the disregard was
put into effect than before.* Earnings, the third factor,

---

*In 1966, 12.9 percent cases were closed for employ-
ment; in 1968, 11.6 percent; and in 1970, 7.2 percent.[3]

were $175.86 per month on average for working AFDC mothers
in 1969 and $221.25 in 1971.[4] Here there is a positive in-
crease of $45.39 per month.

It is difficult to fully understand the significance of
the foregoing data. The proportion of mothers in the "employed" status remained the same, while case closings for
employment declined sharply. Both of these findings are related to each other. A mother is counted as "employed" for
one of two reasons: either she is working and not earning
enough so that AFDC supplements her earnings, or she has
started to work shortly before and is only awaiting a salary
check or some welfare agency administrative action before
her case will be closed. If more mothers were at work after
the disregard than before, this should be reflected in both
those continuously at work and in those who are in the process of being terminated from AFDC. The terminating group
should show up first in the "employed" figure and then in
the "case closings" figure. Even if less cases proportion-
ately are being closed as a result of the higher "breakeven
point" (the point at which income exceeds need and the case
is closed) due to the disregard, then more of these cases
should be reflected in the account of those "employed."
Since the latter is not the case, it would appear that not
only are there no more women at work, but in fact, there may
be less, since the lower case-closing rate does not result
in a higher "employed" rate.

The increase in earnings at first appears significant
as a measure of work effort since it was a substantial increase between 1969 and 1971. This too, however, falls
short of this promise when we note that earnings have been
rising regularly and by large amounts since 1961. Average
monthly earnings went from $54.09 in 1961 to $135.43 in 1967,
to $175.86 in 1969, to $221.25 in 1971.[5] It is difficult
then to attribute this last rise to the effectiveness of the
disregard.

The national data does not appear to lend support to the
thesis that the "thirty and one-third" disregard had a positive effect on work effort. This is even more surprising in
light of the fact that AFDC mothers have become more employable through the years. Both educational and skill levels
have risen. In 1967, for example, 15.9 percent of mothers
had completed high school but had not gone further. By 1971,
this figure was as high as 19 percent.[6] In 1961, 7.7 percent of the mothers were designated as "skilled, blue-collar";
by 1968 fully 26 percent were so listed.[7] Earnings, as already noted, had also risen progressively. Family size, an
important dimension of employability, has also decreased.
From 1967 to 1971 the median number of children per AFDC
family has dropped from 3.2 to 2.8.[8]

Although recipients have become personally more employable, the rising tide of general unemployment could tend to mitigate this factor. The unemployment rate has climbed from 3.5 percent in 1969 to 5.9 percent during 1971.[9]   However, the negative impact of general labor market conditions on AFDC female employment becomes questionable when we note that in 1961 while the unemployment rate was as high as 6.7 percent (higher than 1971) as much as 12.9 percent of AFDC mothers were at work--very close to the 1971 proportion of 13.9 percent.

In summary, we might say that in spite of the increased employability of AFDC mothers, the national data tells us that work effort, as measured by those at work while on welfare and cases closed for employment, had not increased after the institution of the disregard. Although earnings did rise, it does not appear that they rose in relation to the 1967 earnings exemption.

EMPIRICAL STUDIES

The national data consider all the states and yield average results. It is important, therefore, to examine local studies as well, since these may show the differing effects of the disregard in different areas. There have been few empirical studies to test the results of the earnings exemption. Those that were carried out have only recently reported their findings. As in the case of the national statistics, the time period tested was short and so falls prey to the same limitations.

The National Analysts Inc. did a cross-country survey at the request of the Department of Health, Education and Welfare and published their results in May 1972. Two waves of interviews were conducted: the first of 3,508 mothers in ten cities in 1969 when the disregard had been in effect for six months; the second in 1971 of 2,425 of the same women. At the end of the first interview each respondent was given a detailed explanation of the disregard policy so that ostensibly all of them were knowledgeable about it in the period between the first and the second interview.

Since it is essential for AFDC mothers to <u>know</u> about a work incentive in order for it to be effective, knowledge of the disregard was one of the two principal effects that the survey tested. During the first set of interviews almost half of the women were not aware of the earnings exemption and expressed the thought that if they obtained a job that paid as much as the welfare check, they would lose the welfare check entirely. During the second series of interviews, fully one-third of the respondents were still under this

misapprehension, although they had all been informed otherwise by the interviewer.[10]

The fate of work effort fared as badly. During both
waves of interviews the same proportion of women (two-
fifths) were either working, looking for work, or enrolled
in training programs. Only one-quarter of them were actually working at the time of both interviews. When we look at
work motivation as described by the respondents themselves,
the picture is even bleaker. Only 13 percent said they had
looked for work because of the earnings exemption, and less
than half of these said they had started to work because of
the exemption. None of them had left welfare as a result of
the new policy, and fully four-fifths of the women said they
had engaged in no work-related behavior as a consequence of
the disregard.[11]

The study concludes that "for women, at least, the Earnings Exemption had been ineffective in compelling recipients
into the labor force or into job training," and that, "the
Earnings Exemption failed to act as a work incentive for the
population it was designed to motivate."[12] It goes on to
speculate that the lack of a financial incentive is not the
only major barrier to employment in the AFDC population and
that, in fact, it may never have been a barrier for many
recipients.

Not all studies come to so grim a conclusion. The Gary
Appel and Louis Schlenker analysis of work effort in 13
Michigan counties used secondary data and studied the period
between July 1969 and July 1970 in an attempt to test the
effect of the disregard. They found that female employment
did increase during this period from 7 percent to 12.1 percent, a proportion of all AFDC families. In addition, a
longitudinal sample of 3,831 women who were on AFDC in both
July 1969 and in July 1970 was also examined and yielded a
70 percent net increase in employed women between both
times.[13]

While the National Analysts study was concerned with
awareness of the disregard policy, the Appel and Schlenker
exploration was heedful of additional factors. The problem
was to isolate the effect of the earnings exemption in order
to determine whether it was this that caused the increase in
employment. Several barriers are potential to isolating the
effect of the disregard. Such structural dimensions as
knowledge of the disregard; lack of jobs, transportation,
and child care facilities; and poor health would all qualify
employment rates. It is even more difficult to isolate the
effect of the disregard statistically, since the exemption
causes the "breakeven point" to rise, thereby keeping more
employed recipients in the caseload and increasing the

proportion of those employed. What needs to be measured, then, is net _new_ employment to ascertain whether work behavior has increased.

The researchers attempted to differentiate new employment by taking the July 1970 figure of those employed and deducting from that figure those women who would have been off assistance had their earnings been above the earnings level permitted in July 1969. The adjustment reduced the increase in employment in all geographic areas, but in 9 of the 13 areas the increase over July 1969 was still "statistically significant."

This device brought the issue of earnings into focus. Apparently, earnings increased between 1969 and 1970 from $176 to $191 per month. Average earnings increased in 10 of the 13 areas, "but it is unclear whether this is a significant increase caused by the work incentive."[14] As in the national data, case closings for employment fell from 33 percent to 23 percent in the one year, indicating that those with higher earnings were retained in the caseload. Increases in earnings are like increases in employment: it is difficult to separate out higher earnings from the fact that higher earnings are now permissible as a result of the higher breakeven point brought on by the disregard.

Unfortunately, Appel and Schlenker failed to test their results in the context of trend data. Their conclusion that employment rose between 1969 and 1970 because of the disregard is mitigated by examining employment in Michigan prior to 1969. The national HEW surveys present a picture of 10.8 percent AFDC mothers employed in Michigan in 1961, 12.4 percent in 1967, 5.6 percent in 1969, and 9.4 percent in 1971.[15] Apparently in May 1969 when the national survey was taken, AFDC employment in the state was at an all-time low. The fact that it rose after this and did not even reach the proportion in 1971 that it had in 1961 and 1967 seems to give no special credit to the disregard policy. It is difficult, too, to attribute any increase in earnings in Michigan to the disregard since the average monthly earnings continued to rise from $59.32 in 1961 to $129.38 in 1967 to $196.68 in 1971.*[16]

The researchers did, however, take labor market conditions into account in assessing the effectiveness of the disregard. Unemployment in all Michigan areas rose from 1969 to 1970; conversely, AFDC employment also rose. There appeared, by these standards, to be no relationship between

_____

*Earnings in Michigan for 1969 were not included in the national survey.

the general availability of jobs and the degree of female AFDC employment. They then tested "female employment in selected occupations" as a measure of labor market conditions that would be more relevant and found that "pertinent female employment" had actually increased slightly in 5 of the 11 areas, but that the increases in AFDC employment did not correspond to these increases by geographic area. They conclude that "the relationship between the rate of AFDC employment and the measurements of the labor market is ambiguous at best."[17] Despite the expressed ambiguity, Appel and Schlenker summarize: "[In] general, the measures indicate a decline in labor market conditions; therefore, it appears reasonable to restate the claim that the increase in AFDC employment rates occurred in spite of, not because of, changes in labor market conditions."[18] It is clear, however, that relevant labor market conditions ("pertinent female employment") did not decline but actually improved. Surely this should constitute the measure of job availability and consequent effect on AFDC mothers' employment rates.

In spite of uncertainties in the evidence presented and the difficulties in isolating the effects of the disregard on work effort both pragmatically and statistically, Appel and Schlenker conclude that the earnings exemption had a decided, positive outcome in the 13 counties they reviewed in Michigan. Given all these qualifications, the observer is hard-pressed to agree with their conclusion. The results of their analysis can be criticized even more concretely on the grounds that they did not refer their findings to a historical context. The increases in both employment and earnings, when viewed in conjunction with previous trends in employment and earnings in Michigan, do not appear to be due to the disregard.

A more cautiously optimistic survey of statewide, not county, data in Michigan, conducted by the Department of Social Services, looks for the impact of the disregard on the work effort of both AFDC parents.[19] Table 4 lists the percent employed and the average earnings of recipients during every month from July 1969 to December 1971. Vernon Smith and Ayden Ulusan, who reviewed these data, note that employment rose from 10.8 percent to 12.5 percent in the 30-month period. According to their interpretation, the reasons for the drop in employment after May 1970 was (a) the General Motors strike, (b) rising unemployment rates, and (c) a $40 ceiling on allowable work expenses as a welfare policy during the 10-month period from September 1970 through June 1971. They generally agree with Appel and Schlenker that the disregard had a positive effect on work effort during this, its first year of operation.

TABLE 4

Employment and Average Earnings of Michigan AFDC
Recipients, July 1969-December 1971

Month	Percent Employed	Average Gross Earnings
July 1969	10.8	177.00
August	12.1	182.00
September	12.5	184.00
October	13.0	185.00
November	13.7	188.00
December	13.8	187.03
January 1970	13.9	185.56
February	14.0	185.00
March	14.2	186.06
April	14.3	187.16
May	14.4	188.41
June	14.3	191.64
July	14.2	192.85
August	13.7	193.92
September	13.3	188.10
October	12.8	186.01
November	11.9	186.08
December	13.1	186.28
January 1971	12.8	185.27
February	12.6	185.46
March	12.5	184.30
April	12.6	185.38
May	12.7	185.64
June	12.6	187.16
July	12.3	188.40
August	12.2	194.55
September	12.0	197.96
October	12.0	202.10
November	12.3	206.62
December	12.5	209.00

Source: Michigan Department of Social Services.

However, like Appel and Schlenker, these investigators
do not take into account trend data. The 1967 national AFDC
survey shows that in Michigan, female employment alone was
as high as 12.3 percent during that year.[20] In the Smith
and Ulusan study, Table 4 shows that employment of both parents was at a low in 1969 and then started to recoup. But
even by as late as December 1971 it had reached only 12.5

percent--about what it was in 1967. Another point of criticism is the work expense limitation as an explanation of why
there was a drop in employment after May 1970. The limitation ended in June 1971, but there was no subsequent rise in
employment after this time in response to its demise. If a
decrease in incentive created a decrease in work effort as
the study claims, then the reverse should also be true.

Turning from employment to earnings, Table 4 shows that
earnings continuously rose except during the 10-month period
where work expenses were limited. The rise after the 10-
month period is attributed to two factors: when the ceiling
on work expenses was remanded, this "provided an incentive
for increased earnings, and also allowed recipients to remain on assistance at higher wage levels. Together the result has been higher average earnings for persons receiving
assistance. . . ."[21] Again, it is essential to put the data
into a time perspective. Before concluding that the disregard acted as an incentive for higher earnings, it should be
noted that earnings both nationally and in Michigan had been
rising all along, as already cited. The rise in earnings,
therefore, cannot be said to be directly attributable to the
disregard. Conversely, the drop in earnings during the period when the work incentive was lowered can be adequately
explained as a function of the lowered breakeven point (those
with higher earnings were not retained on the caseload) without resorting to "incentive" interpretations.

Thus far, only labor-force participation and earnings
have been the variables studied in testing the effect of the
disregard. Another analysis presently conducted also by the
Michigan Department of Social Services is concerned with
both new employment and continuing employment of AFDC mothers.
Work history and earnings level of mothers in two Michigan
counties on AFDC in July 1969 are considered in three time
periods: (a) 1969-70 (after the disregard), (b) 1968-69
(before the disregard), and (c) 1967-68 (also before the
disregard).

The findings on continuing employment appear encouraging at first. Of those mothers who were employed in July
1969, 57 percent remained employed one year later, whereas
only 44.2 percent retained employment the previous year
(1968-69) when there was no disregard policy. This study,
however, did consider the meaning of trends and examined
also 1967-68 where it was found that employment continued
then almost 60 percent, in the absence of the work incentive.
Smith concludes that for the employed group, "employment behavior appears to have been influenced in a positive direction, but because of the similar experience observed for the
1967-68 period, the positive change cannot be considered one
of great magnitude."[22]

New employment fared better. Of those mothers who were not employed in July 1969, about 10 percent did become employed in the following year as compared with 4.7 percent new employment the previous year and 5.3 percent two years before. In the case of these mothers, "a definite positive change in employment behavior was observed."[23] It is important to bear in mind, however, before attributing this result to the earnings exemption, that the previous survey cited of AFDC employment in Michigan indicated that employment rose between July 1969 and July 1970 but fell after that time. Employment levels of mothers in the two subject counties may also have dropped after July 1970.

The effect of the disregard on earnings in the two counties was neutral according to this analysis. Among those employed between 1969 and 1970, 32.3 percent increased their earnings, whereas in the previous year as much as 42.8 percent increased their earnings, and two years before, 35.4 percent did the same.[24] The findings of the previous study, which indicated that earnings rose between July 1969 and July 1970, can be evaluated more realistically when we observe that this study points out that they rose even more the year before and the year before that.

The empirical studies appear to have contradictory findings and tentative conclusions. Most of them can be criticized for lack of historical perspective. In the absence of controls either of a group nature or of a time dimension, to permit comparison, the positive findings can be interpreted as artifacts. When, in fact, a time perspective is introduced, as in the two-county Michigan study, the data fail to hold up as an indicator of the positive effect of the disregard on work effort.

TAX RATES

In the mid-1960s, when it became apparent that "services" as a strategy for reducing the AFDC caseload had not succeeded, and the question arose of why recipients did not work, a theory of work incentives emerged. It appeared to economists that work in public assistance carried with it a "100 percent tax rate"; that is, for every dollar that the recipient earned, an equivalent dollar was deducted from the assistance payment. It seemed obvious that such rules would inhibit work effort, and in order to promote work among AFDC recipients they proposed measures that would institute work incentives in the form of earnings exemptions. They recommended, in short, that the "tax rate" on earnings be reduced; the 1967 disregard of earned income, effective in 1969, was the first major piece of reform legislation reflecting this theory of "economic rationalism."

Although logical, the idea that up until that time a 100 percent tax rate existed was erroneous. The system simply did not work that way, even theoretically, in most states. Some states paid only a percentage of need to each family and allowed earned income between that base payment and full need (as the state defined it) to go untaxed or disregarded. This was true mainly in the southern states where the payment standard was low to begin with, and which chose to encourage work in this manner.

Tax rates also differed among states as a consequence of the differential treatment of work expenses. Some states included child care and work-related taxes such as social security, while others didn't. Some states had flat allowances for work expenses while others treated this item on an "as incurred" basis. Another type of work allowance was an automatic stipend for employed recipients ($20 per month in Michigan). New York City's variant of this was the basic food allowance that was higher for employed recipients than for others.

But even in those states that, by statute, had mandated a 100 percent tax rate policy, there was a disparity between principle and practice. In 1967, economists N. A. Barr and R. E. Hall did an empirical study of actual tax rates in nine major cities and found that on $100 of monthly earnings the rates at which AFDC recipients were taxed ranged from 18 percent to 72 percent. They surmised that tax rates may have been even lower than these figures indicate since their "results measure the implicit tax rates that caseworkers think they are imposing and may exceed the tax rates as perceived by family members to the extent that they are able to conceal their true earnings from the case worker." They conclude that there are "relatively low tax rates on earned income under AFDC" and that "the prevailing belief that the system of public assistance imposes a nearly confiscatory tax on earnings needs substantial revision."[25]

The image of a 100 percent tax rate uniformly applied in all states was not reality-tested and was hardly a valid foundation for the work incentive "reform" that was legislated in 1967. But what effect did these differential tax rates have on work effort before the disregard was instituted? As early as 1960, Alvin Schorr, evaluating a policy of work for AFDC mothers, noted that in 1958 of 34 states with a maximum payment or other such limitation on benefits, 23 states had an average of more than 10 percent of their mothers working and 11 states had a work average that was less than this. Conversely, of 16 states without a maximum only two states had more than 10 percent working while 14 states had less. He infers that "states that provide this small measure of incentive show an increased percentage of working mothers over those that do not."[26] The incentive in the first group of states was the practice that earnings between the maximum payment and what the state considered the "need standard" were either fully or partially disregarded; tax rates in these states were therefore lower than in the second group of states.

Genevieve Carter, examining the 1961 AFDC survey, pointed to the fact that while the national average of working mothers was 14 percent, in states with an earnings exemption the median was 22 percent, while in states without an exemption the median was only 6 percent. She explains this dramatic difference as follows:

> On the one hand, women on AFDC are highly
> motivated to work when grants are low and
> earnings exemptions are allowed . . . dem-
> onstrating the value of employment incen-
> tives. On the other hand, states that at-
> tempt to meet 100 percent of state stan-
> dards . . . do not have the same high rate
> of employment. . . . Obviously, employment
> incentives such as earnings exemptions for
> life survival have a different meaning from
> employment incentives for upward mobility.[27]

And Irene Cox, reporting on the situation in 1967, showed that the median proportion of working mothers in states with earnings exemptions was 28.3 percent compared with a median of 10.5 percent in other states. She adds, like Carter, that those states with work incentives were "states with relatively low AFDC payments; consequently, economic pressure to acquire additional income was considerable."[28]

Schorr, Carter, and Cox recognized that both incentives and low assistance payments played a part in producing differential work effort among states but did not attempt to evaluate the relative weight of each agent. Furthermore, it is conceivable that other factors also operated to produce more work in low-benefit, high-incentive states such as administrative emphasis on work as a policy, agricultural economics, etc.

When Congress in 1967 legislated the "thirty and one-third" disregard, it was thought of as a standardizing, across-the-board work incentive. The fact is, however, that even after this, earned income was treated differently in different states. The 1967 amendment simply "tacked on" to an already diversified system a stable deduction that did not alter the basic variance. Treatment of earned income or

tax rates on earned income differed after 1969 for basically
the same reasons as before the disregard.

Work expenses still differed. Federal guidelines stipulated that work expenses were to be deducted after the
"thirty and one-third" deduction, but in 1970 less than half
the states were in conformity with this regulation. Child
care expenses differ in the same way: in some states they
are allowed on the budget after the "thirty and one-third"
and in some states before. This difference in methods de-
termines whether all or only two-thirds of these expenses
will be met by the welfare grant.

As Joseph Heffernan points out, "[Another] major source
of unintended variance is the degree of caseworker discretion currently practiced in the administration of public
assistance."[29] Caseworkers can manipulate work expenses
either positively or negatively, and can also ignore or
acknowledge client resources. As Leonard Hausman noted,
"[Some] earnings may go unreported by recipients or ignored
by caseworkers"[30] thus reducing tax rates in these instances. Barr and Hall's findings that tax rates in practice were lower than tax rates in theory can be explained
by caseworker discretion.

The greatest variance in tax rates always was and con-
tinues to be due to the differential disregards of earned
income created by different methods of budgeting this income. There are three basic ways of calculating the welfare
grant when earned income is involved. In 1971 (a) in 35
states payment was equal to need (or some part of need) and
earnings were deducted from what was paid to people with no
income; (b) in 9 states the payment was a maximum amount
while the need was used to determine initial eligibility for
AFDC; earnings between maximum and need were completely disregarded; (c) in 7 states earnings were deducted from need
but only a percentage of the difference between earnings and
need was paid.[31] All three methods apply the "thirty and
one-third" disregard first and then treat "countable income"
(what is left) as earned income to arrive at the amount of
the grant. The tax on earnings is obviously highest in
states that use method (a) where all countable earned income
is subtracted from the welfare grant. It is lowest in
method (b) where all income between maximum and need is disregarded, and in-between in method (c). Robert Lerman summarizes differences in tax rates:

> The tax rates on earnings that AFDC recipi-
> ents face depend on the $30 plus one-third
> Federal regulation, on State maximums, on
> ratable reductions, on State provisions

for disregarding work expenses, and on the
savings and consumption components of allow-
able work expenses. . . .[32]

Just as tax rates still differ among states, so does
work effort. Benefit levels also continue to vary as they
did before the institution of the disregards. We will attempt here to analyze the variance in work effort in relation to tax rates and benefit levels as they operate in 20
states.[33] The 20 states considered are those listed in the
national 1971 AFDC survey. We divided them into "high incentive" and "low incentive" designations according to
whether they use methods (a), (b), or (c) to budget earned
income; (method [c] is considered high incentive). The
benefit level is defined by the "average payment per family" in each state for a family of one parent and three
children; and earnings are the "average monthly earnings"
of the mother in each of the 20 states. The percent employed in each state is expressed as "total," "full-time,"
and "part-time" work. Table 5 shows the results of a least
squares regression analysis using earnings, total work,
full-time work, and part-time work as dependent variables.
Table 6 summarizes the correlation of the same four dependent variables with benefit levels and incentives.*

Table 5 indicates that total work is related positively
to incentives and negatively to benefit levels about the
same degree. The estimated regression coefficients on which
the beta weights are based suggest, furthermore, that when
the dependent variable "total work" is disaggregated into
full-time and part-time work, incentives for full-time work
are statistically more important as an explanatory variable
than benefit levels; for part-time work, however, benefit
levels are more important than incentives. Earnings, if
conceived of as a measure of work effort, would be expected
to rise with higher incentives and lower benefits; instead
earnings rise with higher benefits and are only minimally
affected by incentives. We could conclude, as observers before 1967 noted, that total work rises with high incentives
and low benefits. However, we now know that it is full-time
work that is related more to high incentives, and part-time
work that is related more to low benefits. Earnings are
higher in high-benefit (wealthier) states and do not appear
to be a function or measure of work-effort.

_____

*I am grateful to Lynn Ware for technical assistance in
preparing Tables 5 and 6.

TABLE 5

Linear Regression Analysis (Least Squares) Benefit
Levels and Incentives as Predictors of Earnings,
Total Work, Full-Time Work, and Part-Time Work, 1971

Dependent Variable	Independent Variable	Beta Weight	R^2
Earnings	Benefit level Incentive	+ .84 + .32	.63
Total work	Benefit level Incentive	- .54 + .51	.72
Full-time work	Benefit level Incentive	- .28 + .65	.62
Part-time work	Benefit level Incentive	- .73 + .17	.63

Source: Findings of the 1971 AFDC Study, U.S. Department of Health, Education and Welfare (Washington, D.C., 1971), Tables 21, 56, and 83.

TABLE 6

First Order Correlations of Benefit Levels
and Incentives with Earnings, Total Work,
Full-Time Work, and Part-Time Work, 1971

Dependent Variable	Independent Variables	
	Benefit Levels	Incentives
Earnings	+ .73	+ .05
Total work	- .69	+ .67
Full-time work	- .48	+ .73
Part-time work	- .78	+ .40

Source: Findings of the 1971 AFDC Study, U.S. Department of Health, Education and Welfare (Washington, D.C., 1971), Tables 21, 56, and 83.

But to elicit the effect of the "thirty and one-third" disregard, it would be necessary to separate this from the effects of the "method-of-budgeting" incentives that were present before. Table 7 was devised to look at <u>changes</u> in work and earnings between 1967 and 1971 in the same 20 states. We first note that the high-incentive states in both years have twice as much work in all categories as the low-incentive states. We would have expected, had the disregard been effective, that the gap in work effort between high- and low-incentive states would have narrowed in 1971. In 1967 the low-incentive states had no formal earnings disregard, so that a disregard after that time should have increased work effort in those states substantially more than in states that already had an incentive (the high-incentive states). But in both years the differential in work between high- and low-incentive states remains the same. We would also expect that the low-incentive states would have a greater percentage increase in work between 1967 and 1971 than the high-incentive states since the former had no incentive before. As it is, neither low- nor high-incentive states have an increase in total work and both groups have similar increases in full-time work and decreases in part-time work. Earnings, too, increased by the same percent in both low-incentive and high-incentive states. There is, in effect, no difference in the change in work effort from 1967 to 1971 between low- and high-incentive states.

CONCLUSIONS

After examining the national data, the empirical studies, and the impact of tax rates on work effort both before and after the disregard, we are forced to conclude that the disregard did not have a salutary effect on work effort. This is not to say that work incentives do not produce increased work effort. The difficulty with the "thirty and one-third" is that it was imbedded in an already ongoing incentive system. There have always been work incentives in AFDC. States both formally (through methods of budgeting) and informally (through discretion) provided means whereby some part of earned income could be ignored. It was a mistake, therefore, to define the system as one of "no incentives" before and "incentives" only after 1969, and no surprise to discover that there was consequently no significant increase in work after this date. It is difficult, then, to test the work incentive hypothesis by the lack of positive results of the "thirty and one-third" disregard.

TABLE 7

Changes in Full-Time Work, Part-Time Work, Total Work,
and Earnings 1967 and 1971, by Low-Incentive and
High-Incentive States

	1967	1971
Low-incentive states		
Percent full-time workers	.05	.06
Percent part-time workers	.05	.04
Percent workers	.10	.10
Average monthly earnings		
(average per state)	$126.95	$194.07
High-incentive states		
Percent full-time workers	.10	.13
Percent part-time workers	.09	.07
Percent workers	.19	.20
Average monthly earnings		
(average per state)	$132.02	$201.53

Percentage change 1967 and 1971	Low-Incentive States	High-Incentive States
Full-time work	+20	+30
Part-time work	-20	-22
Total work	00	+05
Earnings	+53	+52

Sources: Findings of the 1967 AFDC Study, Tables 38
and 99, and Findings of the 1971 AFDC Study, Tables 21 and
56, U.S. Department of Health, Education and Welfare (Washington, D.C., 1970 and 1971).

Another factor that curtailed the effect of the disregard was the existing pattern of full-time and part-time
work. At first glance, it might seem that full-time work
increased as a result of the disregard since 7.5 percent of
AFDC women worked full time in 1969 and 8.3 percent did so
in 1971. But the fact is that 6.6 percent were in this
category in 1967 and 4.6 percent were full-time workers in
1961,[34] illustrating a continuing trend to full-time work.
An explanation of this trend (in line with our findings that
incentives have a positive effect on full-time work) is (a)
the continuously increasing formal incentives starting with
work expenses in 1962, and (b) expanding areas of discretion
that lead to greater informal incentives. The disregard, an

additional formal incentive, did not accelerate the rate of increase in the trend to full-time work. The corollary decrease in part-time work, which is also a trend since 1961, can be explained by rising benefit levels, a pattern even in the southern states where most of the part-time work took place. As benefits continued to rise, part-time work continued to fall, and the efficacy of the disregard was diminished.

Thus the three factors most directly related to incentives that have mitigated the effect of the disregard are (a) incentives both formal and informal that existed before, (b) the continuing trend to full-time work that was part of an increasing and cumulative incentive system, and (c) the pattern of decreasing part-time work within a context of increasing benefit levels.

The two latter factors have resulted in a tension between rising incentives and rising benefits, which has tended to cancel out any potential increase in total work. The "thirty and one-third" disregard policy and later welfare reform proposals tried to resolve this dilemma by instituting incentives that were thought to be high enough to offset high benefits. This strategy, in turn, presents its own problems as it tends to increase caseloads by increasing "breakeven" points and keeping people on welfare. A more viable policy, given the goal of work, might be one of attaching incentives to the job market rather than to the welfare system. By creating more rewarding jobs, the incentive-benefit dilemma might be avoided to some degree.

NOTES

1. Findings of the 1969 AFDC Study, U.S. Department of Health, Education and Welfare (Washington, D.C., 1970), Table 19.
2. Reasons for Opening and Closing Public Assistance Cases, U.S. Department of Health, Education and Welfare (Washington, D.C., 1969), Table 9; Reasons for Discontinuing Money Payments to Public Assistance Cases, U.S. Department of Health, Education and Welfare (Washington, D.C., 1972), Table 4.
3. Reasons for Opening and Closing Public Assistance Cases, U.S. Department of Health, Education and Welfare (Washington, D.C., 1966), Table 9; Reasons for Opening and Closing Public Assistance Cases, U.S. Department of Health, Education and Welfare (Washington, D.C., 1968), Table 9; Reasons for Discontinuing Money Payments to Public Assistance Cases, U.S. Department of Health, Education and Welfare (Washington, D.C., 1970), Table 4.

4. Findings of the 1969 AFDC Study, op. cit., Table 61; Findings of the 1971 AFDC Study, U.S. Department of Health, Education and Welfare (Washington, D.C., 1971), Table 56.

5. Characteristics of Families Receiving Aid to Families with Dependent Children, November-December 1961, U.S. Department of Health, Education and Welfare (Washington, D.C., 1963), Table 50; Findings of the 1967 AFDC Study, U.S. Department of Health, Education and Welfare (Washington, D.C., 1970), Table 99.

6. Ibid., Table 40; Findings of the 1971 AFDC Study, op. cit., Table 23.

7. Perry Levinson, "How Employable Are AFDC Women?" Welfare in Review 8, no. 4 (July-August 1970): 13.

8. Findings of the 1967 AFDC Study, op. cit., Table 5; Findings of the 1971 AFDC Study, op. cit., Table 6.

9. Monthly Labor Review, "Current Labor Statistics," [1969-72] (Washington, D.C.: U.S. Department of Labor).

10. National Analysts, Effects of the Earnings Exemption Provision upon the Work Response of AFDC Recipients (Executive Summary), U.S. Department of Health, Education and Welfare (Washington, D.C., 1972), p. 17.

11. Ibid., pp. 20, 21.

12. Ibid., pp. 21, 25.

13. Gary L. Appel and Robert E. Schlenker, "An Analysis of Michigan's Experience with Work Incentives," Monthly Labor Review 94, no. 9 (September 1971): 18.

14. Gary Louis Appel, Effects of a Financial Incentive on AFDC Employment (Minneapolis: Institute for Interdisciplinary Studies, 1972), p. 88.

15. Findings of the 1967 AFDC Study, op. cit., Table 38; Findings of the 1969 AFDC Study, op. cit., Table 19; Findings of the 1971 AFDC Study, op. cit., Table 21; Characteristics of Families Receiving AFDC, op. cit., Table 23.

16. Appel, op. cit., Table 50; Findings of the 1967 AFDC Study, op. cit., Table 99; Findings of the 1971 AFDC Study, op. cit., Table 56.

17. Appel, op. cit., p. 66.

18. Ibid., p. 67.

19. Vernon K. Smith and Ayden Ulusan, The Employment of AFDC Recipients in Michigan (Michigan: Department of Social Services, 1972).

20. Findings of the 1967 AFDC Study, op. cit., Table 38.

21. Smith and Ulusan, op. cit., p. 9.

22. Quotation from letter from Vernon K. Smith, Director, Division of Income Maintenance and Employment Research, State of Michigan Department of Social Services, March 2, 1973.

23. Ibid.

24. Ibid.

25. N. A. Barr and R. E. Hall, "The Taxation of Earnings Under Public Assistance," Working Paper No. 85 (Cambridge: Massachusetts Institute of Technology, Department of Economics, April 1972), p. 19.

26. Alvin Schorr, "Problems in the ADC Program," Social Work 5, no. 2 (April 1960): 9.

27. Genevieve Carter, "The Employment Potential of AFDC Mothers," Welfare in Review 6, no. 4 (July–August 1968): 9.

28. Irene Cox, "The Employment of Mothers as a Means of Family Support," Welfare in Review 8, no. 6 (November–December 1970): 15.

29. Joseph Heffernan, Jr., Variations in Negative Tax Rates in Current Public Assistance Programs: An Example of Administrative Discretion (Madison: University of Wisconsin, Institute for Research on Poverty, 1972), p. 7.

30. Leonard J. Hausman, "Cumulative Tax Rates in Alternative Income Maintenance Systems," Income Transfer Programs: How They Tax the Poor (Washington, D.C.: U.S. Congress, Joint Economic Committee, 1972), p. 114.

31. "States' Methods for Determination of Amount of Grant for an AFDC Family Size of Four as of 12/71" (unpublished table, U.S. Department of Health, Education and Welfare, March 31, 1972).

32. Robert I. Lerman, "Incentive Effects in Public Income Transfer Programs," in Income Transfer Programs, op. cit., p. 15.

33. The high incentive states are Missouri, Tennessee, Mississippi, Georgia, Florida, California, Washington; the low incentive states are Illinois, Massachusetts, Michigan, Louisiana, Alabama, Pennsylvania, Kentucky, North Carolina, Maryland, Texas, Ohio, New York, New Jersey. "Average payment per family" is obtained from Table 83; "average monthly earnings" from Table 56; percent employed total, full time, and part time from Table 21 in Findings of the 1971 AFDC Study, op. cit.

34. Characteristics of Families Receiving AFDC, op. cit., Table 23; Findings of the 1967 AFDC Study, op. cit., Table 38; Findings of the 1969 AFDC Study, op. cit., Table 19; Findings of the 1971 AFDC Study, op. cit., Table 21.

CHAPTER
5

WORK REQUIREMENTS: WIN

In 1935 when Aid to Dependent Children was introduced in Congress as a proposed part of the Social Security Act, the Senate Finance Committee then defined ADC children as those "in relief families which will not be benefited through work programs or the revival of industry."[1] However, in 1967 Congress appeared to take a definitive step in the direction of work for AFDC recipients and instituted a requirement "that all states establish a program for each appropriate AFDC adult and older child not attending school with a view to getting each of them equipped for work and placed on jobs."[2] They thus created the Work Incentive (WIN) program that was to be mandatory in all states.

From 1935 until 1962, despite various attempts on some states' part to encourage or require work from AFDC recipients, the federal government showed little interest in this issue. In 1961, however, the Social Security Act was amended to include unemployed parents (UP) in the ADC Title IV on a temporary basis, and in 1962 the UP provision was renewed for an additional five years. This provision allowed fathers into the program for the first time, thereby adding employable adult recipients to what was essentially a group outside the labor market. These men were, without a doubt, expected to find work as a condition of their eligibility. In 1961 they were to be registered with the state employment agency, in 1962 Congress established grants to the states for Community Work and Training programs that were optional on the states but compulsory for UP fathers wherever they existed; refusal to participate in work and training led to jeopardizing the entire family's eligibility for AFDC.

The 1967 amendment that made AFDC-UP permanent contained, in its early versions, proposals for renewing the

Community Work and Training programs (CWT) and making them mandatory on the states. But, as passed, CWT was converted to WIN, a much broader effort at putting AFDC recipients to work and, for the first time, was to include mothers. While the origin of work for AFDC recipients can be found in the UP provision (the inclusion of men into the AFDC program), the impetus to focus on work for AFDC mothers (the bulk of recipients and till now considered basically unemployable) came from other sources. The conversion of CWT to WIN was not accidental. It emanated from a Congress that was intent upon holding down the continuing growth of the AFDC caseload and that was disillusioned with the 1962 panacea of services. WIN was conceived as a strategy to contain that growth by putting each appropriate AFDC recipient to work.

But although the WIN amendment had stipulated that all appropriate individuals be involved in work and/or training, and the large majority of these were women, WIN, in fact, did not have the intended effect on AFDC mothers in regard to work. An important reason for this was congressional am-bivalence. One set of tensions concerned the place of com-pulsion in modern, liberal social policy. To reach its goal of constraining AFDC growth, the great majority, if not all employable and potentially employable AFDC recipients, would have to be compelled to enter the WIN program. The liberal democratic tradition called, instead, for individual choice and an ideal of individual growth. Initially, the Committee on Ways and Means had recommended "the enactment of a series of amendments to carry out its firm intention of reducing the AFDC rolls by restoring more families to employment and self-reliance, thus reducing the Federal financial involve-ment in the program."[3] However, the amendment as passed spoke of WIN creating "a sense of dignity, self-worth, and confidence which will flow from being recognized as a wage-earning member of society."[4] The two goals of reducing the AFDC caseload and providing opportunities for individual growth were already in conflict at this early stage.

If individual growth was at issue for everyone, its conversion to "the welfare of the family and the children" for mothers was inevitable. Congress was loath to jeopar-dize this consideration (the well-being of children) in an effort to compel mothers to work. Financial constraints also imposed limitations on congressional intent. Congress was not prepared to spend the huge amount of money that would be required to put every feasible individual through an elaborate system of training and into the labor market. This was especially pertinent in the case of mothers who re-quired high-cost day care services before they could be com-pelled to participate in WIN.

So that despite the determined rhetoric about work, the ideological constraint of liberalism and the practical problem of cost led Congress to qualify in practice what it had espoused so vigorously in principle. To modify the pragmatic immensity of involving so many recipients in the WIN program and the political unfeasibility of compelling mothers to work, three features were built into WIN that had the effect of mitigating the compulsory aspects of the legislation, especially for women. The concepts of selectivity of who was appropriate for WIN, of differentiation among participants as regards work and training needs, and of sanctions to enforce work norms all tended to soften the overtly harsh requirements inherent in WIN.

Had the WIN program emerged as it had originally been envisioned, it would have strongly affected the work-welfare choice. Through enrollment in WIN, great numbers of AFDC mothers would have been impelled into the labor force. As it was, the processes of selectivity, differentiation, and sanctions acted to keep the program small and ineffectual.

SELECTIVITY

If all adult recipients were to be trained or employed through the WIN program, this would entail at least the 1,320,448 parents included in the 1,278,223 families on AFDC in 1967, not considering the children over 16 years of age.[5] In April 1970 the national total of authorized WIN slots was only 120,000.[6] Clearly a way had to be found to eliminate over 1,200,000 recipients from consideration for WIN. Congress took the first step in what was to be an ongoing constriction policy by setting up categories of persons that the states would not be permitted to refer to WIN.

The persons who could not be referred to WIN according to the 1967 amendments were the ill, incapacitated, aged, and those too removed from a WIN project to participate; those attending school full-time; and those whose substantially continuous presence in the home was needed because of the illness or incapacity of another member of the household. However, a person requesting referral must be referred unless the welfare agency determined that it was not in the best interests of the individual or the family. Aside from these restrictions, the decision about who was appropriate for referral was left to the state, to be implemented by the welfare agency. The legislation also specified that the welfare agency was responsible for assuring child care arrangements to all those mothers who were involved in the program.

As the state welfare agencies were given the power to
decide who would be referred, the Department of Health, Education and Welfare took an active position in interpreting
the legislation as it saw fit. Through the WIN guidelines,
it established "priority-of-referral" groups that the states
should adhere to. The order of priority was as follows:
unemployed fathers on AFDC-UP; children over age 16 who
were neither at work nor in school; volunteer mothers who
did not have preschool-age children; volunteer mothers who
did have preschool-age children. But the guidelines went
beyond this order of priority and stipulated that only two
of these groups must be referred to WIN: fathers and children over 16. Mothers, in effect, were not included. By
thus eliminating all mothers from required participation in
WIN, HEW severely restricted the intent of the WIN amendment
and put all female adult participants in the class of volunteers.

The federal guidelines also eliminated from WIN mothers
whose participation would endanger the family's well-being
(a determination that the caseworker in the welfare agency
was to make) and mothers to whom the welfare agency could
not provide adequate child care. That these criteria operated in practice is evidenced by the fact that in 1969, of
those not found inappropriate for referral, 10 percent were
because child care arrangements were not available while an
additional 20 percent were because the mother was "required
in the home because of age or number of children."[7] By 1972
these figures were even higher, being 25 percent and 21 percent respectively.[8] Almost half of assessments at this time
were not referred to WIN for reasons of child care.

Both the legislation and the federal guidelines had
drastically reduced the number of participants (especially
mothers) in the WIN program. The states even further delimited the potential WIN population. Through fiscal year 1971,
2.7 million assessments had been made and only 24 percent of
these were found to be "appropriate for referral" to WIN.
Only 79 percent of those appropriate were referred, and less
than 60 percent of these were actually enrolled.[9] Because
they were inhibited by the 20 percent financial contribution
they had to make to the program, the states decreased the
number of WIN slots the federal government had created. Of
the 120,000 authorized slots in April 1970, there were only
89,445 enrollments nationwide.[10] Although slots were increased in 1971, only 109,000 enrollments had taken place.[11]
The states also narrowed participation in WIN by putting
their own restrictions on who should be referred. Massachusetts, for example, prohibited from involvement with WIN
"mothers of children under three years of age who do not
voluntarily enroll."[12]

Still another force limiting the wide application of WIN was the caseworkers in local welfare agencies. Since it was they who, in the last analysis, decided which of their clients were to be referred to WIN, their discretionary power was enormous. The Auerbach study clarifies this:

> The situation where a caseworker reviews all his cases in terms of a clear set of eligibility criteria for WIN, and refers according to priorities . . . is almost non-existent. . . . The effect is to make a fortuitous relationship between client and caseworker as much of a factor in screening and assessment as the guidelines and eligibility requirements.[13]

Since caseworker discretion loomed so large, their attitude in regard to employment is crucial. Joel Handler and Ellen Jane Hollingsworth, among others, have documented a negative view toward work for AFDC mothers and pointed out that it is basically a "social work decision" that is made jointly between the recipient and the caseworker about work. The decision is based mainly on familial and personal factors and is individualized, rather than made as an expression of welfare policy.[14]

As a result, according to the Auerbach corporation, "although each state has developed referral priorities in its guidelines, and most caseworkers have these guidelines at their disposal, priorities for other than mandatory unemployed fathers are not closely adhered to."[15] The usual procedure was that "the caseworker makes the mandatory referrals and then usually selects volunteers from among those he is currently in contact with."[16] According to caseworkers, "the most eligible candidates are those who are motivated, interested, young, able to secure child-care services, and have had at least some high school. Interest and motivation" tend to be primary.[17]

As for AFDC mothers, voluntary referrals took precedence in most states. Levitan, Rein, and Marwick note that "although participation has been made mandatory in some states for mothers with suitable child care arrangements, in most states mothers participate only voluntarily."[18] Evidence of voluntary participation is provided by the William Reid and Audrey Smith study of 318 AFDC mothers in WIN which notes that one-half of their respondents had initiated their own referral.[19] This practice of voluntary rather than mandatory referral of mothers, no doubt, in part stems from both the difficulty and the expense of meeting the child-care requirement of the federal legislation and from explicit HEW policy as exemplified in the WIN guidelines: "It would be acceptable, and in fact desirable, for states to make referral voluntary for mothers of young children and perhaps for those with older children who express a strong feeling that they are needed at home to take care of the children."[20]

The voluntary nature of female participation is further illustrated by the ratio of females to males among WIN enrollees. During its beginning year (1968) only 46 percent were mothers, by the end of 1969 58 percent were mothers,[21] and by 1970 this figure had climbed to 71 percent of WIN enrollees.[22] The slight predominance of men at the beginning was, no doubt, due to the legislative clause giving men priority and more stringently enforced at the start of the program than later on, when women began to volunteer in greater numbers. In 1971 the female proportion dropped to 62 percent, and by 1972 to 53 percent.[23] This occurred because the unemployed parent segment of AFDC in which the father is present doubled in numbers between 1969 and 1971 as a result of the economic recession. In 1969, AFDC-UP families were 75,500 and comprised 4.6 percent of the total AFDC caseload, while in 1971 there were 152,600 such families being 6.1 percent of all AFDC cases.[24]

The degree of participation of AFDC mothers in WIN was directly tied to how important it was for men at any given time to use WIN services. Mandatory referrals (men) came first; whatever slots remained after that were accorded to mothers who were mainly volunteers. Since, basically, men and volunteers filled the less-than-numerous slots available, the matter of compelling AFDC mothers to work never really became an operative issue.

Reliance upon a principle of selectivity had the effect of diminishing the compulsory features of WIN for AFDC mothers. By setting limitations on referral, Congress had legislated certain restrictions on its own dictum that all employable recipients should participate in WIN. HEW, creating the WIN guidelines for the states, interpreted the legislation in such a way as to even further narrow congressional qualifications. Some states, in turn, also delimited the WIN population; and caseworkers in local welfare agencies, through discretion in the referral process, desisted from involving mothers in the program. This funnel of selectivity, comprising several levels of legislative decree and practical operation, narrowed to the end of almost eliminating compulsory work and training for female heads of households who in 1969 accounted for over three-quarters of all AFDC families.

DIFFERENTIATION

Another principle that affected the work-welfare choice for AFDC mothers was differentiation. Selectivity had factored employable recipients into priority-of-referral groups. Those women who had made it through the selectivity process and become enrollees were further segmented or differentiated into job-readiness groups through the mechanism of WIN program components. These components were used in such a way as to weaken the goals of job training and jobs for participants, thereby creating neither a restriction of the work-welfare choice through compulsion nor an expansion of this choice through the acquisition of skills and work opportunities.

Differentiation was based on the premise that the AFDC population was comprised of persons who were at different levels of readiness for work, a premise that derived, in turn, from the notion that all recipients were beset with formidable barriers to employment. This belief was part of the "pathology syndrome," an explanation offered for why AFDC recipients do not work. Although pathological barriers had by now come to include personal-structural as well as psychological problem areas, the perspective of impediments residing in the person remained unaltered. The WIN enrollee, therefore, was encompassed by a host of such impediments, not the least of which was thought to be an innate recalcitrance to work, all of which had to be overcome in order to make him or her job-ready.

Since the flaw was in the individual, individual treatment was required; the professional social work strategy of "starting where the client is" became the base method for achieving differentiation. Corollary to this was the underlying professional doctrine of the uniqueness and worth of every individual (participant). The ideology of individualism embracing both respect for the individual and a concept of individual barriers to employment led to a "service" philosophy: service _to_ the enrollee rather than an obligation _from_ him to work.

The service idea led to a focus on rehabilitation rather than on jobs. Professional attitudes, ensconced in a liberal political context, were leery of the bogus of compelling people (mainly mothers) to work. And, since it seemed that each WIN participant needed specialized assistance to overcome his particular barriers, that assistance became highly diversified and therapeutic. In addition, a focus on jobs would have entailed the necessary availability of a great many jobs, and jobs, at least the kind that WIN preferred for its enrollees, were just not there. WIN's avowed purpose was "training with a future"[25] and "career-ladder" rather than dead-end, low paying jobs.

The method by which differentiation was achieved was the use of WIN program components. In order to effect the complex goal of starting where each participant was, a giant superstructure, replete with several subdivisions and housing many different components, was erected. The First Annual Report of the Department of Labor lists these program components: Intake and Assessment Phase, Orientation, Exploration by Job Tryout and Job Sample Methods, Prevocational Training Workshop, Other Prevocational Training, Basic Education and General Educational Development, Institutional Vocational Training, Other Manpower Training Programs, Holding Between Program Components, On-the-Job Training, Public Sector Employment, At Work and Receiving Intensive Follow-Up Services, and At Work and Receiving Regular Follow-Up Services. Enrollees could theoretically fit into any one of these program levels at any given time depending upon their special needs. Everyone had to go through Intake and Assessment, and Orientation.

The WIN components can be clearly divided into two categories: those that were job-oriented such as Institutional Vocational Training, Manpower Training, On-the-Job Training, Public Sector Employment, etc., and those that were not job-oriented such as Orientation, Prevocational Training, General Educational Development, etc. If AFDC mothers in WIN would have made significant use of the job-related components, their opportunities for entry into the job world would have been greatly enhanced. But accounts of WIN have pointed out heavy concentration of WIN enrollees in the nonjob-related components and much less focus on the others.

A report prepared by the Department of Labor for Congress lists the number of enrollees in each component as of April 30, 1970: a full 60 percent of them were in the non-job-related components.[26] Reid and Smith reported that out of 124 women WIN enrollees they interviewed in three different cities, 48 percent were in educational courses (mostly high school) and only 14 percent in job-training courses; a full 35 percent were in "holding" (between components) status.[27] The Auerbach study similarly found that as much as 46 percent of enrollees were in basic education, only 25 percent were in institutional training, and another 25 percent in prevocational or vocational training. Only 40 percent were sent to job interviews. It was concluded that "the more job-oriented the component, the less likely it is that the enrollee will be in it."[28]

In addition, each enrollee (no matter at what level of job-readiness) had to go through a lengthy orientation period where he was introduced to "the world of work" and was made "aware of those attributes other than job skills required to obtain and hold a job."[29] Even those immediately employable received supportive services such as counseling. David Franklin, in a California study of 360 enrollees, found that the WIN counselors themselves thought that 20 percent of their enrollees could have been immediately placed on a job, while another 36 percent "perhaps" could have been placed as soon as they entered WIN.[30] Nevertheless, they were all processed through the WIN training components.

Structurally, much of the WIN program content was not job oriented. The results of this bias can be clearly demonstrated by the outcomes of WIN participation. While the final goal for each enrollee was explicitly asserted to be a job, in fact, very few participants achieved it. As of December 1970, there were 23,691 people who successfully completed WIN (employed for from three to six months after obtaining a job); this was 10 percent of enrollees (and only 1 percent of assessed recipients). By April 1972, 61,500 out of 385,131 enrollees or only 15 percent were in this category.[31] Thus, a small proportion of enrollees obtained and kept jobs for a minimum of three months. How these jobs were procured is also significant. The Auerbach study revealed that only one-half of those who obtained jobs actually did this through WIN; the other half got their own jobs.[32]

Auerbach Associates, recognizing the nonjob orientation of the WIN program components, recommended that there be more focus on job development, increased utilization of on-the-job training, and greater use of special work projects. Congress, too, aware of the poor job success rates in WIN, in 1971 amended the Social Security Act, allocating one-third of WIN expenditures beginning in fiscal year 1973 to on-the-job training and public service employment—two highly job-oriented WIN components.

WIN acted like a funnel in that it initially selected out very few of the AFDC women who might have participated, thus leaving mostly volunteers. For those who did participate, through the principle of differentiation of program components, it implemented a highly individualized and rehabilitative focus that constricted work training and work options. Many, therefore, did not receive job training adequate to the task of obtaining and keeping jobs. Its effect on the work-welfare choice was almost nil: it neither compelled mothers to work through an emphasis on work training and work, nor did it enhance the opportunities for work to any appreciable extent for those women who wanted to work.

In spite of congressional caution and ambivalence regarding work for AFDC mothers, a major intent of the WIN amendment referred to mothers, the huge majority of adult recipients. The logical way to implement such a goal was through compelling mothers to participate, and the strategy most applicable to compulsion was sanctions for noncompliance. However, the WIN program did not effectively use sanctions to enforce participation for either men or women.

To begin with, the WIN sanctions as dictated by the legislation were mild. Whereas the predecessor Community Work and Training programs (addressed to men) had called for closing an AFDC case and depriving the entire family of assistance should the adult refuse participation, WIN was not so reciprocal in its sanctions. Only the individuals referred and not accepting the referral, or in the program and then refusing to continue, both "without good cause" were to be deleted from the AFDC family budget. This was true, however, only after a 60-day counseling period (by the welfare caseworker) wherein the recalcitrant recipient was to be persuaded to comply. During this period, both the refusee and his family continued to receive their usual welfare payment, only it was to be paid to someone else as a "protective payment" and/or directly to vendors (of food, rent, etc.) instead of to the family. If after 60 days of counseling the referred person still was not willing to participate in WIN, he would be deleted from the budget but the family would continue to receive protective or vendor payments for as long as the case was otherwise eligible.

Under these sanctions the family would be penalized in two ways: its AFDC check was to be reduced by the amount of the referred person's share, and at least part of what it did get would be controlled by someone else. Notwithstanding these chastisements, the WIN sanctions were very mild. In effect, the head of an AFDC household, though considered employable, was not constrained from not working to support his family since his family would continue to receive AFDC support; the case was not closed. Some states modified even these sanctions. Massachusetts, for example, had a 60-day period to allow the recipient to file an appeal against WIN referral, which preceded the 60-day counseling period during which no punitive action was taken. There were, therefore, 120 days of grace in all. In addition, great precaution was taken during the entire process to insure that the recipient was given every opportunity to comply, and that there was, indeed, no good cause for him to refuse:

Should the determination be made that an individual is appropriate for referral to the
WIN program but refuses to accept referral,
the social worker will further evaluate the
recipient's suitability for referral, drawing upon the social study, and will reassess
the recipient's motivation for participation
in the program. In those cases in which referral is mandatory, the social worker will
assist the recipient in working through his
feelings about mandatory referral and explain to the recipient the penalties for refusal and notify the recipient in writing of
his right to appeal such a determination.[33]

Not only were the legislative sanctions mild, they were
not frequently implemented. The Auerbach report finds that
sanctions were never really applied. Caseworkers said they
did not have the time to do counseling and "the use of a protection and vendor payment is virtually unworkable." The
study reported that "in most areas, including the largest urban areas, the number of applicants who had their benefits
legally removed was a minute portion of those referred, despite the fact that thousands of de facto refusals had occurred."[34]

The General Accounting Office reported on the use of
sanctions in Los Angeles and Denver. In Los Angeles, out of
107 fathers who refused to participate, the father's share of
the welfare budget was discontinued in only 55 cases. In Denver no payments had been reduced through July 1970 although
94 fathers had refused to participate in WIN.[35] California's
county welfare departments said they "found the sanctions cum
bersome and time-consuming for their limited staffs and imposed them on very few enrollees terminated from WIN without
good cause."[36] Welfare agencies also were reluctant to apply
sanctions because they saw them as resulting in hardship to
the family.

Wherever sanctions were applied in this limited way, the
were applied to men. Men were, after all, the only substantive mandatory category. The Unemployed-Parent amendment to
AFDC stipulated that the father be referred to work or training within 30 days of receipt of assistance. This, coupled
with HEW guidelines that discouraged referral of mothers, lef
fathers as the only major group of compulsory referrals, and
the only one to which sanctions were technically relevant.

Since women were volunteers, sanctions were theoretically not applicable and since there were more volunteers
than WIN openings or slots, there was no pragmatic need to
apply them. The General Accounting Office points out that
in both California and Colorado, sanctions were only appli-

cable to fathers. Jon Goldstein, writing for the Joint
Economic Committee, states that "the penalty does not apply
to mothers who volunteer for WIN. Since most of WIN's clientele are volunteer mothers, the sanctions are largely a
fiction."[37] Levitan, Rein, and Marwick add: "[In] most
states mothers participate only voluntarily, and therefore
are free to leave without penalty. . . . mothers constitute
over half of WIN enrollment, but no sanctions are provided
against most of them."[38]

Sanctions for noncompliance with WIN requirements were
mild, infrequently used for fathers, and not applied in the
case of mothers. What were the outcomes of this in terms of
participation in WIN? The official figure of refusals to
participate after referral by the welfare agency is 10 percent. This, however, is questionable, since through June
1971 an additional 12 percent did not report for scheduled
interviews and another 21 percent were turned back as either
"unsuitable" or "unacceptable."[39] The actual proportion of
referrals who were not enrolled because of refusal to participate without good cause may then be as high as 43 percent,
or at least 22 percent. Another point in the WIN process at
which sanctions were relevant was after enrollment when the
individual decided to "drop out" of the program--again "without good cause." Of all enrollees "leaving before comple-
tion" through March 1970, 15.5 percent "refused to continue," 3.1 percent were "separated by administrative decision," and 6.5 percent "could not be located."[40] Thus as
many as 25 percent left WIN without good cause after having
been enrolled.

These relatively high refusals and dropout rates are
not differentiated by sex in the official statistics.
Whether it was the unemployed fathers or the mothers who
created them is pertinent. An analysis of the HEW figures
for the last quarter of 1969, where refusals to participate
without good cause are delineated by state, shows that among
the 21 states listed that had an Unemployed-Parent program,
the average number of refusals per state was 66, whereas
among the 21 states that did not have such a program, the
average was 6 per state.[41] This simply means that over ten
times as many refusals to participate in WIN came from
states where fathers were among the referrals as came from
those states where only mothers were referred. Since in
1969 over half of all enrollments were mothers, the "ten
times" figure is even more impressive as an indicator of the
fact that the great preponderance of refusals were men. Men
in WIN also had higher dropout rates than women. The Analytic Systems study found that only 18 percent of female
terminees dropped out without good cause as opposed to 22
percent male.[42] Women not only volunteered for WIN, they
participated more and stayed longer than men.

Just as selectivity had not compelled AFDC mothes to
enter the work and training requirements of the WIN program,
and differentiation had not compelled them to jobs, so sanctions in WIN did not compel them to participate. The sanctions were legislatively mild and essentially not implemented. Since most female referrals were voluntary, sanctions were especially not applied to them. It appears that
many women did not refuse to participate, whether volunteers
or not, but a sizable amount (18 percent) dropped out of the
program after being in it for a while. This last could be
because the program was disappointing in its lack of job
focus or because child care or other such personal problems
became barriers to participation. Sanctions, as they were
practiced in WIN, did not have the effect of compelling AFDC
mothers to work. Thus, they, in consonance with the prin-
ciples of selectivity and differentiation, left the work-
welfare choice free of constraints and unaffected by the WIN
program.

CONCLUSIONS

In essence, WIN did not constrict the work-welfare
choice for AFDC mothers. Women were neither compelled to
participate in WIN--mothers became the WIN volunteers, nor
compelled to remain in WIN--if they had elected to participate. Only a small proportion of AFDC mothers were in the
program: in 1969, 4.1 percent of all AFDC mothers were enrolled and 2.2 percent were awaiting enrollment after referral. Even if all those referred became enrolled this was
only 6.3 percent of the mothers.[43] In 1971, only slightly
more--6.8 percent of all mothers--were either enrolled or
awaiting enrollment.[44] Within WIN, program content was such
that it did not substantively focus on obtaining and holding
jobs--on actual work--and in this sense it also failed as a
compulsory program. Thus, by virtue of its small size, its
voluntary nature and its nonwork-oriented design, WIN left
intact the prevailing work-welfare choice for AFDC mothers.
By the same token, WIN did not expand this choice either. Although the program was voluntary for mothers and so
consisted of a highly motivated clientele, it did not, in effect, lead to any substantial increase in the job-obtaining
and job-holding capacity of its enrollees; only a small proportion of participants actually became involved in work as
a result of contact with WIN. Auerbach Associates further
postulate that the "post-WIN employment behavior of WIN enrollees is nearly unaffected by participation in WIN. The
dominant influences on the long-term employability of WIN

enrollees appear to be the enrollees' initial capacity, their involvement with the low-wage, unstable labor market, and comparable value of welfare financial assistance."[45] With only 6 to 7 percent of AFDC mothers involved in WIN, it could not have become a significant resource and enlarger of options for those women who did want to work. A small proportion of all AFDC mothers partook of WIN services, a much smaller proportion of them obtained work through WIN, and it is alleged that even for those women, success in work experience could not be attributed to WIN.

It should be remembered that congressional intent was to make it possible for every employable adult recipient to engage in work or training; the WIN funnel yielded only a trickle of this vast potential population. WIN, then, can be seen as a case of the failure of public policy to implement its own work requirements and as a prototype of the difficulties encountered in this kind of endeavor. Perhaps the most important reason for this failure was Congress' own ambivalence. Both ideological and financial restraints propelled Congress to institute certain safeguards to insure that humane as well as economically beneficial goals would be honored. The resulting tension between these goals defeated the primary objective of enforcing work requirements.

Since there was no enforcement, freedom of choice for AFDC mothers prevailed. They chose not to work at jobs that could not compete with welfare status. The Reid and Smith study of mothers in WIN found that

> the jobs they appeared to want would probably have had to provide them with an income clearly better than they would receive on AFDC or with an activity intrinsically more interesting and gratifying than staying at home. Low-paying, unskilled jobs might offer them little more, if not less, than they already had.[46]

Despite the best efforts of WIN to provide "career-ladder" jobs, the market did not afford such opportunities for these women, especially at times of high unemployment. The "thirty and one-third" earned income disregard instituted in 1967, which raised the "breakeven point" (case-closing level), also acted to curtail working at low-paying jobs. The decreasing welfare stigma and increasing in-kind benefits had made the receipt of AFDC less unattractive and the desire to lose this status less pressing. Even among those women who did elect to participate, Reid and Smith found that only 15 percent were in WIN because of a desire to get off welfare.

The remainder were equally divided between wanting to increase their income and wanting the "psychological" benefits
of work.[47]

Had the WIN program clearly been a work-incentive effort, incentives in the form of jobs that were competitive
with welfare status should have been available. Had it been
a work-requirement program, it should have been less exclusive in whom it included and used more sanctions to enforce
participation. Its ambivalence prevented it from both being
and doing either. Although Congress did not forsake its ambivalence, neither did it give up on the idea of work as a
strategy for reducing the AFDC caseload. The 1971 amendment
that reemphasized on-the-job training and special work projects was an effort to reaffirm this dictum. In 1972, Congress passed the Talmadge amendment (see Chapter 6) in a
still further and more intense effort to reverse the direction of the WIN program and institute work requirements for
AFDC recipients.

NOTES

1. Social Security Amendments of 1971, U.S. Senate,
Committee on Finance, Hearings (Washington, D.C., 1972),
p. 1309b.

2. Social Security Amendments of 1967, U.S. House of
Representatives, Committee on Ways and Means, Report
(Washington, D.C., 1967), p. 96.

3. Ibid.

4. Stephen F. Gold, "The Failure of the Work Incentive
(WIN) Program," University of Pennsylvania Law Review, 119,
Comment (January 1971): 487.

5. Findings of the 1967 AFDC Study, U.S. Department of
Health, Education and Welfare (Washington, D.C., 1970),
Table 6.

6. Reports on the Work Incentive Program, U.S. Department of Labor and U.S. Department of Health, Education and
Welfare (Washington, D.C., 1970), p. 78.

7. Ibid., p. 180.

8. Assessments Completed and Referrals to Manpower
Agencies by Welfare Agencies under Work Incentive Program
for AFDC Recipients, U.S. Department of Health, Education
and Welfare (Washington, D.C., 1972), Table 5.

9. Sar A. Levitan, Martin Rein, and David Marwick,
Work and Welfare Go Together (Baltimore: Johns Hopkins University Press, 1972), pp. 93, 94.

10. Reports on the Work Incentive Program, op. cit.,
p. 76.

11. Levitan, Rein, and Marwick, op. cit., p. 76.

12. State Letter 242, The Commonwealth of Massachusetts, Department of Public Welfare (October 1968), p. 4.

13. Reports on the Work Incentive Program, op. cit., p. 246.

14. Joel F. Handler and Ellen Jane Hollingsworth, The "Deserving Poor" (Chicago: Markham, 1971), Chapter 6.

15. Reports on the Work Incentive Program, op. cit., p. 248.

16. Ibid., p. 246.

17. Ibid., p. 248.

18. Levitan, Rein, and Marwick, op. cit., p. 96.

19. William J. Reid and Audrey D. Smith, "AFDC Mothers View the Work Incentive Program," Social Service Review 46, no. 3 (September 1972): 351.

20. Reports on the Work Incentive Program, op. cit., p. 229.

21. Ibid., p. 176.

22. Levitan, Rein, and Marwick, op. cit., p. 79.

23. Ibid., and Assessments Completed and Referrals to Manpower Agencies, op. cit., Table 3.

24. Findings of the 1969 AFDC Study, U.S. Department of Health, Education and Welfare (Washington, D.C., 1970), Table 13 and Findings of the 1971 AFDC Study, U.S. Department of Health, Education and Welfare (Washington, D.C., 1971), Table 15.

25. Gold, op. cit., p. 497.

26. Reports on the Work Incentive Program, op. cit., p. 76.

27. Reid and Smith, op. cit., p. 356.

28. Auerbach Associates, An Impact Evaluation of the Work Incentive Program, Vol. I (Philadelphia, 1972), p. 1-18.

29. Vernon K. Smith and Ayden Ulusan, The Employment of AFDC Recipients in Michigan (Michigan Department of Social Services, 1972), p. 29.

30. David S. Franklin, A Longitudinal Study of WIN Dropouts: Program and Policy Implications (Los Angeles: Regional Research Institute in Social Welfare, 1972), p. 8.

31. Jon H. Goldstein, The Effectiveness of Manpower Training Programs: A Review of Research on the Impact on the Poor, Studies in Public Welfare, Paper No. 3 (Washington, D.C., 1972), p. 52.

32. Auerbach Associates, op. cit., p. 1-15.

33. State Letter 242, op. cit., p. 5.

34. Reports on the Work Incentive Program, op. cit., p. 260.

35. Problems in Accomplishing Objectives of the Work Incentive Program, U.S. General Accounting Office (Washington, D.C., 1971), p. 34.

36. Ibid., p. 23.
37. Goldstein, op. cit., p. 51.
38. Levitan, Rein, and Marwick, op. cit., p. 96.
39. Ibid., p. 95.
40. Reports on the Work Incentive Program, op. cit., p. 39.
41. Ibid., p. 181.
42. Analytic Systems, Analysis of WIN Program Automated Termination Data, [Department of Labor contract No. 53-49-70-02] (1970), p. 27.
43. Findings of the 1969 AFDC Study, op. cit., Table 19.
44. Findings of the 1971 AFDC Study, op. cit., Table 21.
45. Auerbach Associates, op. cit.
46. Reid and Smith, op. cit., p. 353.
47. Ibid.

6

WELFARE REFORM:
FROM WORK INCENTIVES
TO WORK REQUIREMENTS

Just as the failure of the 1962 strategy of services as a means to contain the AFDC caseload had given rise to the initiation of the WIN program, so the apparent ineffectiveness of WIN provided fertile ground for still another attempt to stop the growth of the AFDC rolls by increasing work effort: welfare reform. The Senate Finance Committee, referring to WIN, had said, "Operations under the program . . . have been disappointing, and it has had almost no impact on soaring welfare rolls." From the inception of WIN in July 1968 until July 1971, the number of families on AFDC had increased by 1,169,000.[1] Nor had the "thirty and one-third" earned income disregard any discernible effect on the size of the AFDC caseload.

The president's statement in 1969 summed up the general disillusion with AFDC: "[Whether] measured by the anguish of the poor themselves or by the drastically mounting burden on the taxpayer, the present welfare system has to be judged a financial failure." The essential problem was one of growth that manifested itself in several ways. The concrete signs of failure included (a) continuously expanding numbers of recipients, (b) heavy concentrations of recipients in high-paying northern states, mostly in the large cities, (c) family breakup and illegitimacy as increasing reasons for AFDC eligibility, and (d) growing inability of states and cities to finance AFDC. Added to this mélange of specific phenomena was a climate in which national poverty had become an unacceptable and eradicable state of affairs, and in which the rights of the poor had become a prime aspect of the general liberalization of political and social thought.

The basic solution to these problems and the context wherein all other reforms could be effected was the nationalization of the welfare program dealing with assistance to families with children. A national system (as opposed to grants-in-aid to states) would provide more financial aid to the states and more fiscal control. Variations in state benefits, which were thought to cause migration to higher-paying states, would be eliminated, and benefits in high-benefit states would be lowered or kept in check to defray costs, while benefits in low-benefit states would be raised to help alleviate poverty; more equity would thus prevail. The system would be not only more equitable but also more efficient, less discretionary, and less destructive of the rights of the poor.

Nationalization, for this last reason, would also be a more appropriate framework for the second major aim of welfare reform: the inclusion of the working poor. In the current system, inequities exist between the working poor and the welfare poor. Welfare benefits are now higher in many states than the wages paid to those in the potential welfare population who work, thus jeopardizing the principle of "less eligibility" (those on welfare should receive less in benefits than those who receive the lowest wages for working). A further inequity between the working population within AFDC and the working population outside AFDC is a result of the 1967 "thirty and one-third" disregard, which permits recipients to exempt part of their earned income and be eligible for welfare supplementation, while those outside the system with the same earnings are not eligible for supplementation.

These inequities violate a sense of justice, but far more important, they are thought to be a major cause of the rise in welfare. If the welfare poor are "better off" than the working poor, it seems rational that the working poor would opt for welfare status. Including the working poor in the reform of the welfare system would eliminate this hazard. Including the working poor would also help to raise many people above the poverty line by supplementation of wages through welfare. In addition, giving the working poor a subsidy would even out the inequity between them and the welfare poor and thus prevent family breakup for higher income.

There remains yet another crucial flaw in the present welfare system to reform: the apparent lack of work effort on the part of AFDC recipients. Although 1967 had legislated both work requirements through WIN and work incentives through the "thirty and one-third" earnings exemption, these measures had yielded such poor results that clearly this problem had not been resolved. The solution appeared to lie in both stronger work requirements and stronger work incentives and was central to the idea of welfare reform. The double strategy of giving welfare to the working poor to keep them working and eliciting work from the welfare poor to get them off welfare was designed to contain the growth of the "pure welfare" caseload. It was hoped that through these mechanisms people would eventually end up in the category of "work only" or, at the least, the "welfare only" group would diminish.

THE FAMILY ASSISTANCE PLAN

Provisions

The Family Assistance Plan (FAP), first introduced by the president in late 1969 and known in its final form as the Family Assistance Act of 1970, was the first piece of major legislation proposed under the aegis of "welfare reform." In its initial stages there was a $1,600 per year "floor" or guarantee for a family of four ($500 per adult and $300 per child), and a 50 percent tax rate on earned income over $720 per year.

All adult individuals had to register with the Department of Labor (DOL) for work or training provided they did not fall into the following specified categories: persons ill, incapacitated or aged; children aged 16 to 21 attending school; persons needed at home to care for an ill person; mothers in families where father registers; mothers of children under six years of age. The manpower program would be jointly administered by the Department of Health, Education and Welfare, which would provide child care and other supportive services, and the Department of Labor, which would be responsible for work and training. Recipients would receive $30 per month for training. All recipients would register with the DOL if they were not exempted by the above, and the DOL would determine whether they refused to accept suitable work or training, whereupon any person who refused could lose his FAP benefit, although his earnings (if any) would be budgeted; his family, however, would continue to receive its share of the grant, which would be dispensed through a protective payee.

This seemingly simple format of FAP housed severe problems, and the proposal went through many changes within the administration and within congressional committees. Its most obvious failing was in terms of the adequacy of the guarantee: $1,600 for a family of four was not enough for a family to survive on if the head did not work to augment this income. Even more telling, 42 states were paying more

than this to their four-person AFDC families. The first
meaningful change, then, was to increase this base to $2,400
by the use of an $800 per year food stamp subsidy. The tax
rate remained at 50 percent and the "break-even" point (the
point at which benefits would stop) at $3,920.

Another problem, however, soon became evident. Even
with the $2,400 benefit guarantee, many states were still
paying more under AFDC, a fact that liberal interest groups
and congressmen could not abide. AFDC, which FAP originally
was to abolish, now became a program of FAP supplementation
through the state welfare agencies. States that had higher
payments would have to supplement FAP up to these benefit
levels for AFDC families and AFDC-UP families (where AFDC-UP
did not exist, it was to be created). States could not
erode the 50 percent FAP tax rate, but they could tax up to
67 percent (like the "thirty and one-third") beyond the FAP
break-even point.

Unfortunately, the addition of food stamps and state
supplementation, while solving some problems, created new
ones. The combination of food stamps, state supplements,
Medicaid, income and social security taxes, and public housing cumulated the tax rates to very high levels and also
caused the "notch" effect--that is, a family would suddenly
lose almost all its in-kind benefits at one point of increased earnings. The inclusion of AFDC-UP into the state
supplement plan created an inequity between those working
male heads of families who would be getting the supplement
and FAP (they had to work only part time to be eligible for
UP) and those who were working full time and would get only
the FAP benefit.

To solve the notch problem, FAP was revised to include
in-kind benefits (housing, food stamps, and medical benefits)
that were reduced gradually as earnings increased. However,
this strategy produced, in turn, even higher tax rates.
Robert McNown estimates a tax rate of from 75 to 87 percent
in this version of FAP.[2] To solve the inequity problem,
AFDC-UP was removed altogether from state supplementation,
leaving an even greater inequity this time between the
broken family headed by a woman who would receive both FAP
and the state supplement and the male-headed, intact family
that would receive only FAP.

Work Requirements

Congress was disillusioned with the poor success rates
of WIN, both in terms of the small size of the program and
the small proportion of enrollees who had obtained jobs. A

major impetus to reform, therefore, was to create a program that would remedy this failure and actually get recipients to work. One way to do this was to strengthen work requirements.

Many legislators saw HEW as the culprit that had implemented the work requirements in WIN in a "soft" way and thereby destroyed their effectiveness. Joel Handler points out that Congress felt that HEW was holding back in referring recipients to the employment services. State welfare agencies were also thought to be refraining from applying sanctions to WIN enrollees who did not comply, partly as a result of HEW influence. To solve this problem, FAP tried to eliminate HEW from the gatekeeping role for recipients both entering and leaving the manpower cycle. While the state welfare agencies would still mechanically do the referring to the work program, "the Secretary of Labor would, under his own priorities for the selection of recipients, assure the development of an employability plan for each individual registered with the employment office."[3] (Emphasis added.)

At the other end, "the Department of Labor decides who has refused to work. After such a decision a reduction in payment is automatic," according to the Senate Finance Committee hearings on FAP.[4]

Closely allied to Congress' effort to eliminate the lack of administrative rigor that characterized the WIN program was a resolve to eliminate caseworker discretion from FAP. This was to be accomplished through a more specific wording of the work requirement in the federal statute. Whereas the WIN legislation had specified that all "appropriate" individuals register for work, the FAP proposal said that all adult recipients, except those who fell into the specific exempt categories, had to take part in the program. Thus, "a Federal interpretation of who is exempt eliminated the role of the social workers in the State welfare agencies in determining this work test."[5]

Perhaps the most significant step taken to strengthen FAP work requirements was the dictum that mothers with all their children over six years of age had to register for work and training. The WIN legislation made no such restriction, leaving this matter to the states. In terms of priority of referral, in WIN mothers had a low priority with the result that HEW regulations called for only fathers and teenagers to be mandatory referrals. Since the huge bulk of AFDC adults was mothers, FAP tried to prevent this from occurring again.

Finally, FAP legislation harbored the concern that penalties for noncompliance with WIN were too meager and not enforced, and remedied this by specifying what were considered to be stronger penalties this time around. Just as in WIN, the refusee's benefits were to be deducted from the grant and the family paid through another party. But in FAP the income (if any) of the employable person who did not comply was to be considered part of the family income and the grant reduced accordingly; this last was not so in WIN. Most important, however, as a means to strengthen penalties, was the exclusion of the welfare agency as a sanctioning agent; now, if the DOL decided that a recipient had not cooperated, his grant ostensibly would be <u>automatically</u> reduced (after the appropriate waiting period).

Despite FAP's valiant attempts to upgrade requirements, most of them fell short of any real distinction from the WIN program. Putting referrals and sanctions in the hands of the DOL did not insure a "harder" stance in regard to work. Handler points out that although

> HEW and some State welfare agencies interpreted the statute in such a way that only relatively few AFDC recipients were required to be referred . . . at the same time, the Department of Labor through its guidelines for accepting referrals, in effect took the position that if AFDC recipients did not want to accept work or training, they should be excused from the work test.[6]

In addition, workers in the state employment agencies were prone to as much discretion as social workers in the welfare agencies, specifically around the concept of what kind of work was to be considered "suitable" for which kind of clients. Penalties for noncompliance still hinged on this discretion. Sanctions, as in WIN, were mild since only the employable adult and not his family was to be denied a grant. In fact, AFDC penalties, had they been enforced, would have been harsher since at least in 42 states the AFDC grant was higher than the $500 FAP benefit that would be lost. Even the most stringent requirement that mothers of children over age six register for work and training loses some of its bite when it is realized that in 1971, 75 percent of AFDC mothers had children under six, thus leaving only 25 percent subject to the FAP work requirement.[7]

Work Incentives

In its original form, FAP had a low benefit level ($1,600 annually for a family of four) and a tax rate on

earnings of 50 percent, which was lower than the AFDC tax
rate of 67 percent. Low benefits and high incentives produce greater work effort (as was seen in Chapter 4). A low
benefit, however, was not consistent with previous benefit
levels in AFDC (which in the great majority of states were
higher), not adequate for survival in those cases where no
work effort ensued to supplement it, and not politically
feasible in an era of liberalization. The benefit level
was, therefore, raised through the strategies of food stamps
(a benefit in-kind) and state supplementary grants.

Raising the benefit or guarantee had several consequences. First, it raised the break-even point so that more
families were eligible and those who were eligible received
higher grants. This greatly increased the cost of the program, a strong factor in determining its political feasibility. Raising the benefit also raised the tax rate because
an in-kind benefit (food stamps) now added its taxes on
earned income, because state supplements were to be taxed
at a higher rate than FAP (67 percent), and because the
break-even point became high enough for many families to be
required now to pay federal income and social security taxes.
State supplementation, in addition, created inequities among
the states since states were supposed to supplement up to
the level they were at before FAP, and they all had varying
benefit levels. Inequities were also generated by state
supplementation between the working poor who were not eligible for it and the welfare poor who were.

FAP was plagued by the dilemma of what Robert Smith and
Joseph Heffernan call the "uneasy triangle": the inability
to provide adequate benefits, keep costs low, and assure low
tax rates, all at the same time.[8] When FAP raised its benefits, it also raised its cost (which made it unacceptable to
Congress in the final analysis) and increased its tax rate.
By so doing, it defeated the basic purposes of welfare reform, which were to produce equity between states and between the working and the welfare poor, and to increase incentives for work. Incentives, as embodied in the FAP tax
rate, evolved to being lower than the incentives in AFDC.

H.R.1

After several revisions, the Family Assistance Plan
proposal was defeated in the Senate Finance Committee in
1970. The following year, a modified version of FAP called
H.R.1 was introduced in a further effort to effect welfare
reform. The thrust of this proposal was to attempt to remedy the flaws inherent in FAP, especially the trichotomous
predicament of incentives, adequacy, and costs.

Perhaps the most radical innovation in welfare policy since the inception of the Social Security Act was H.R.1's effort to separate the employables from the unemployables, or to distinguish "voluntary" from "involuntary" poverty. Recipient families would be categorized into two groups: those with an employable member would become part of the Opportunities for Families (OFP) program; those without an employable person would go into the Family Assistance Plan (FAP II). To make certain that HEW "discretion" would not again subvert the purposes of "workfare," Congress assigned OFP completely to the Labor Department, including the responsibility of that department to supply day care and all other supportive services necessary for work and training.

The historically difficult task of ascertaining who among the poor are able to work apparently did not faze Congress, which set up the same categories that FAP did delineating employability, with one major exception. This time, mothers of children under six years of age were also excluded from the necessity to register but only until July 1974, at which time only mothers of children under three were excused. This provision made a significant difference in the proportion of mothers currently in AFDC who would be subject to work and training under H.R.1, compared to FAP's 75 percent with children under age six. In 1971 only 37 percent had children under age three,[9] thus leaving a sizable 63 percent open to the requirement. Aside from including such a large part of the AFDC population (80 percent of the families were headed by a mother), H.R.1 called for giving referral priority to mothers and pregnant women under 19 years of age so that "they would not be condemned to a life on welfare."[10]

To make it possible for all these AFDC mothers to work or train, H.R.1 authorized the large sum of $750 million for child care in the first year of operation, $92 million more than FAP had authorized.[11] In addition, child care costs per family of up to four members could now be disregarded up to $2,000 per year. For both women and men, $800 million was to be allocated to public service employment for those who did not fit into the private market, and there was to be a strong focus on on-the-job training, as opposed to the education orientation of WIN.

The penalty for noncompliance with the work and training program was increased from a final $500 in FAP (it was initially $300) to $800 in lost benefits in H.R.1. Although both the FAP penalty and the H.R.1 penalty are equivalent to the yearly benefit for one adult recipient, the increase is, nevertheless, a real one as it might just as easily have been adjusted to remain the same.

In summary, H.R.1 took a much stronger line than FAP on work requirements: it selected employable recipients as targets for work and training; it divested HEW (the "soft" agency) of almost all its referral, sanctioning, and service powers; it pointedly made the majority of AFDC recipients (the "welfare poor") prone to the work-test; and it increased work over training, as well as increasing the penalty for malingering.

Work Incentives

Whereas FAP's guarantee was $1,600 plus $800 in food stamps for a family of four, H.R.1 raised the floor to $2,400 in cash. This, in turn, raised the break-even point to $4,140, thus increasing the cost of the program since each family would receive more, and more families would be eligible. Nevertheless, despite the greater adequacy of the grant, 30 states still paid more to an equivalent family on AFDC. Again, the idea of state supplements to make up this difference was introduced, but this time there was less interest in adequacy than at the time of FAP and the state supplementary provisions were less rigorous. States could supplement or not as they wished under H.R.1; the federal government would not contribute to these programs unless they were federally administered, but states had an option on this. However, if these programs were to be carried out federally, the working poor would not be eligible for them. This, of course, left inequities between states even greater than in FAP as some states would elect to have supplements while others would not; and the disparities in treatment between the working poor and the welfare poor still remained.

The tax rate in H.R.1 was 67 percent after the same yearly $720 disregard as in FAP. Since the FAP rate was only 50 percent, H.R.1 contained a considerable increase in taxes on earned income. Again, state supplements plus in-kind benefits brought the tax rate well above the present 67 percent in AFDC. Henry Aaron estimates that in the range of earnings between $720 and $6,120 per year, cash assistance would have carried a tax rate of 90 percent while cash plus Medicaid and housing yielded a huge 130 percent tax rate.[12] Similarly, Sar Levitan, Martin Rein, and David Marwick point out that under H.R.1 in Chicago a family earning $2,000 per year would have a net income with Medicaid and housing of $6,607, while a family earning $6,000 would end up with only $6,205.[13]

In addition to strengthening work requirements, H.R.1
raised the benefit level (over FAP) and then lowered the
FAP incentive in an effort to maintain "reasonable" costs.
Between FAP and H.R.1 there was already a shift from incentives to requirements as a strategy for implementing work.
H.R.1 did not pass the Senate; tellingly enough, the large
allocation for public service employment did become law in
that year.

THE LONG PLAN

Provisions

In early 1972, Senator Russell B. Long of Louisiana,
chairman of the Senate Finance Committee, introduced his
version of welfare reform that was, indeed, radically different from both FAP and H.R.1. As in H.R.1, the Long proposal differentiated the recipient population into two
groups: families with an employable member and families
with no employables. The employables were to be eligible
for a new, totally federally financed and administered program called the Guaranteed Job Opportunity program to be
implemented by a newly created agency, the Work Administration, while families with no employable member were to remain in the state-administered AFDC programs where they had
been until now.
Employable family heads in the Work Administration were
to be eligible for three types of income-maintenance: (a)
those who could not obtain jobs in the private sector would
be guaranteed jobs by the government at the hourly rate of
$1.50 and could work up to 32 hours per week, thus earning
a total weekly income of $48; (b) those in the private sec-
tor working 40 hours per week and earning under $2.00 per
hour were entitled to wage supplementation of three-quarters
of the difference between their hourly rate and $2.00 per
hour; and (c) those whose total family incomes were under
$4,000 per year would be granted a 10 percent work bonus,
tapering off to zero percent at $5,600 per year. Anyone
working part time in private employment could apply to the
Work Administration for additional work up to 40 hours per
week. The Work Administration would also contain a Bureau
of Child Care that would be authorized to provide day care
to mothers in the employment program. For 1973, $800 mil-
lion would be allocated for this purpose. There would also
be a training program for those who volunteered, but the
rate of compensation here would be $1.30 per hour as op-
posed to the $1.50 that the Guaranteed Job Opportunity

110

program would pay. The novelty of the Long plan lay in (a) guaranteed job opportunities by government, and (b) no benefit at all for employable family heads if they did not work.

When a family had a total income of over $5,600, it was no longer eligible for the federal employment program. States, however, could supplement such a family (or a family having less of an income and in the employment program) if they so desired, but the federal government would participate financially in the state programs only up to $2,400 for a family of four; the states, therefore, would be supplementing employables at their own expense. If they did choose to do this, they would have to disregard earnings from the employment program from $200 to $375 per month-- that is, not tax them--so that the employment program incentive structure would not be eroded. On the other hand, whether the recipient was earning that amount or not, states would have to assume that he or she had earnings of $200 per month, again not to weaken the federal incentive.

Families without an employable member would have an entirely different fate under the Long bill. They would continue to receive AFDC, a state program that, as always, would be partially federally financed. A base grant of $2,400 for a family of four would be guaranteed for them if eligible; some states would pay more than this (as they do now) but again, at their own expense. All states would have to pay at least as much as this in benefits.

Those required to be eligible for AFDC would be (a) a family headed by a mother with a child under age six, (b) a family headed by an incapacitated father, (c) a family headed by a mother who is ill, incapacitated, or aged, (d) a family headed by a mother too remote from an employment project to participate, (e) a family headed by a mother attending school full time regardless of the age of the children, and (f) a child living with neither parent but living with a caretaker relative. There were to be no work requirements for the AFDC group at all; a mother with children under six years of age, however, could volunteer for the employment program. As such, she would be treated like an employable and $200 of monthly income would be assumed. As for any mother who would wish to remain on AFDC (if she had children under six) and work, there would be a flat $20 per month disregard of her earned income.[14]

Work Incentives

For employables, incentives in the Long plan were very different from AFDC, FAP, or H.R.1 incentives. The greatest

incentive to work is, of course, the incentive to live.
The proposal had this concept at its base, in the sense
that if there was no work, there was no benefit at all.
The benefit level (which has an impact on work effort) in
this case was 0 and should have had a 100 percent effect on
creating the initial impetus to work. Once that inevitable
decision was made, the Long plan provided for wage subsi-
dies and a wage bonus as further incentives, but always in
relation to further work effort. Since the base was 0, any
attempt to work more did not reduce an already existing
benefit, simply because there was no such benefit to start
with. In addition, there was an incentive to go from one
type of subsidy to the more lucrative one. Work with the
Guaranteed Job Opportunity program would net less income
than low-paying work in the private sector, which, in turn,
would yield less income than higher paying jobs in the
market.

    Although there was no benefit erosion at the lower end
of the earnings scale, since the Long plan did entail a subsidy that was phased out by higher earnings, there was some
point at which a tax rate set in. This tax started at a
higher earnings level than in the other plans and, therefore, was nonexistent for a very large group of low-wage
workers. From 0 to $3,000 of annual earnings, the negative
tax rate was 10 percent (a negative tax rate is a subsidy);
from $3,000 to $4,000 the tax rate jumped positively to 70
percent; from $4,000 to $6,000 it remained at about 40 percent; and from $6,000 to $8,000 it was about 20 percent.[15]
However, again, with the addition of state supplements,
Medicaid, and housing, the tax rate climbed rapidly. "Tax
rates would have remained somewhat below those called for
in H.R.1, but would still have exceeded 100 percent at
points."[16] But even with the inflation of in-kind benefits,
the tax rate between 0 and $2,500 was a low 20 percent, sub-
stantially lower than in AFDC, FAP, or H.R.1.

    While working fathers and mothers of children over age
six were subject to low (or no) benefits and high incentives, mothers of children under six in the AFDC program
would be the recipients of (relatively) high benefits and
low (or no) incentives. Should a woman in this program
want to work part time (about half the mothers who work in
the current AFDC program work part time), she would have a
net disregard of $20 per month with no allowance for work
expenses--the old 100 percent AFDC tax rate. She could not
resolve this dilemma by opting for the employment program
since there, whether she earned it or not, $200 of income
would be budgeted. Since fully half of the children of
mothers in the WIN program were under six years of age in

1972,[17] these provisions could have become problematic for a great many potentially working mothers.

Work Requirements

Work requirements in the traditional sense were lacking in the Long plan. The basic "requirement" was that all those who were deemed employable should work. Although this was true also in H.R.1, that requirement was, in essence, only a requirement to register for work; since work was not guaranteed, there was a great deal of flexibility between registration and work. A guarantee of work in this plan eliminated that leeway. Recipients of H.R.1 would get benefits, though considered employable, without working; employable recipients of the Long plan would not.

The one potential exception in the Long plan to the mandate that all employable recipients need work in order for the family to receive benefits was the provision for "children of mothers refusing to participate in the employment program." If such children (aged over six) were found to be suffering neglect, the Work Administration would pay the family for one month while the mother received counseling and other services to persuade her to participate. If she was not deemed incapacitated and still did not cooperate with the Work Administration, "the State could arrange for protective payments to a third party to ensure that the needs of the children are provided for."[18] This stipulation sounds very much like the penalties for noncompliance legislated in WIN and proposed in FAP and H.R.1. The WIN penalty was not enforced (see Chapter 5). The Long plan took some precautions to see that its penalty would be. First, it applied only to mothers, unlike the others; it can be assumed, therefore, that if a father were not to participate, the entire family would be penalized. Secondly, the implementation of the penalty would require an administrative shift from the Work Administration to AFDC-- the family would have to be transferred from the federal program to the state program. The noncompliant individual under these circumstances would become very visible, and any sanctions that needed to be taken and were not, very evident. It is, therefore, conceivable that these penalties would be both more enforceable and more difficult not to enforce than their equivalents.

In summary, the Long proposal for welfare reform was based on different premises than its predecessors. Its benefit structure derived not from need (family size was not taken into account) but from work effort. As such, traditional work requirements were not needed to initiate work in the first place. Work incentives in the form of tax rates also had a different meaning; since they were for the purpose of _increasing_ work rather than _initiating_ it, they could start at a higher point on the earnings scale. The Long plan could thereby reach more low-income families at a lower cost to government. In this sense, the plan would have created a more income-redistributive mechanism than the previous plans had. The Long plan, together with other modified versions of H.R.1, was defeated in the full Senate in late 1972. Many observers felt that this signified the end to one era of attempts at welfare reform.

THE TALMADGE AMENDMENT

In the midst of the deliberations and defeats of the various proposals for welfare reform, a proposal for amending Title IV of the Social Security Act (AFDC) "was added to an otherwise minor bill by the Senate during a sparsely attended session. . . . It was accepted today (December 14, 1971) by the House after virtually no debate."[19] This amendment, introduced by Senator Herman Talmadge of Georgia, was essentially a work requirement tacked onto the current AFDC program with some modifications in financing and procedure.

Some proponents of welfare reform, discouraged over the apparent impossibility of getting reform through Congress, managed instead to put through the Talmadge amendment, the explicit purpose of which was "to improve the WIN operation." The 1967 WIN program had obviously failed to accomplish its purpose of putting AFDC recipients to work in order to contain the growth of the AFDC rolls. In WIN, the definition of who was appropriate for referral had been left to the states, and states had different stipulations regarding this. In addition, a great deal of discretion was either delegated to or permitted the welfare agencies that, in turn, passed on some of this discretionary power to the individual caseworkers. As a result, referral practices varied from state to state, from agency to agency, and even among caseworkers. Some states referred a great deal of recipients to WIN, while others referred very few. In addition, it was the perception of some congressmen that volunteers for WIN (mothers) were not given enough attention and were kept waiting while mandated but not-so-willing participants "clogged" the program.

To remedy the poor results of state implementation of WIN, the Talmadge amendment specified that _all_ recipients

of AFDC had to register for work and training, with some
specified exceptions. The only categories exempted from
registration were children under age 16 or attending school;
those ill, incapacitated, or of advanced age; those so remote from a project as to preclude participation; those car-
ing for a member of the household who is ill or incapacitated; a mother in a family where the father registers; and
a mother of a child under age six. To supplement these
stipulations, the Talmadge amendment, unlike the WIN legislation, also specified priorities of referral: unemployed
fathers were to have first priority for work and training;
mothers who volunteer would have second priority; mothers
and pregnant women under age 19 were next; then followed
children over 16 who were not in school; and all other persons. This amendment was, thus, different from WIN in that
it mandated referral for all with specified exceptions and
mandated priorities. It also gave high priority to volunteers.

     The Talmadge amendment, like FAP and H.R.1, sought to
reduce the role of HEW. As in WIN, all supportive services
such as child care, social services, health services, and
vocational rehabilitation were to be supplied by HEW. The
difference lay in the referral process. Recipients were
automatically to register with the Department of Labor
(unless they fell into one of the exempted categories),
rather than to be referred by the welfare agency to the
manpower agency. Essentially, the welfare agency still had
the responsibility, in practice, both to prepare the enrollee and to supervise his entry to the program. Still
not certain that welfare would (this time) cooperate in
this endeavor, Congress specified that a state had to make
certain that at least 15 percent of its registrants did end
up at the manpower agency, or federal funding would be reduced accordingly.

     This time, federal matching was increased to 90 per-
cent for all services, while federal participation in WIN
had been 80 percent for manpower services and 75 percent
for child care and other social services. In line with the
recommendations of the Auerbach report on WIN, the Talmadge
plan stipulated that states must allocate at least one-
third of their funds to public service employment and on-
the-job training "reflecting a clear preference for real
jobs as opposed to long-term classroom training."[20] In addition, employers who hired WIN enrollees were to be given
substantial tax credits as an inducement to provide these
opportunities.

     Penalties for noncompliance for recipients were like
those in WIN. After a 60-day counseling period, if the

registrant was still not willing to work with the manpower agency, he or she was deducted from the AFDC budget, while the family continued to receive a grant. Voluntary registrants could withdraw at any time without penalty. If a recipient wished to contest the decision to remove him from the benefit schedule, he or she could "have a fair hearing process available at every step from appraisal to job referral."[21]

The Talmadge amendment went into effect in July 1972. The time period, therefore, in which to look for trends or measure success is extremely short. Even so, Leonard Hausman ventures that "casual, but widely held, impressions are that the FAP work requirement, embodied in the Talmadge amendments (now in effect) in fact is having little or no impact."[22] A "Second Quarterly Report" of the DOL reviews the first six months of operation. During this time 580,000 persons registered (1.5 million had been expected to register in fiscal year 1973), and 185,000 of these became participants in the program. Of the 185,000, 60,000 were placed on jobs (this is one-tenth of registrants and one-third of participants).[23] For the first nine months of the program, there were 1 million registrations; 256,678 of these were certified as able to work, and there were 82,075 job placements.[24]

These figures are similar to the job-attainment rate in WIN: Auerbach Associates had reported that 37 percent of enrollees obtained jobs on their own or through WIN.[25] It is even more striking that out of the sizable numbers of registrations in the Talmadge procedure, only from one-fourth to one-third were considered for referral to the program. Since Congress had so carefully specified those who need to participate in the law itself, one wonders why the "slippage" between registration and referral and is reminded of the narrowing process of the WIN "funnel." It seems clear, even at this early date, that participation falls short of the rigorous standards intended by the amendment. There were only 82,000 job placements out of a possible 1.5 million employables.

A local evaluation of the Talmadge operation in New York City is even more telling. The study sample was comprised of Home Relief, AFDC-UP, and AFDC recipients and covers the period March through June 1972.* Only 8 percent of these actually received a job placement, while 20 percent

---

*New York City started the Talmadge procedure before its effective date as part of a demonstration project along these lines.

116

received at least one referral but could not secure a job. Of the participants, 56 percent never received a referral of any kind whether for a job or for training.[26] Summing up a larger period of time, the study concludes: "At least in its first year of operation, the program appears to have directed far fewer people into the labor market than the cost and scale of the operation merits."[27]

Some of the same implementation problems that plagued the WIN program seem to have emerged in Talmadge, too, and may help account for some of these failings. The Senate Finance Committee reviewed implementation plans shortly before the effective date of the amendments. One area of difficulty noted was the continuing lack of cooperation between HEW and DOL in creating joint regulations as required by law. Another was the complicated procedure that was projected for registration of recipients. Contrary to the letter of the amendment, people were to be registered with the welfare agency and then sent back and forth between welfare and DOL. The Committee comments:

> Apart from the question of the apparent disregard for the intent of Congress that the recipient register with the Labor Department, this paper shuffling seems to delay for a considerable period of time the ability of the employment service to put a job-ready individual to work.[28]

A New York _Times_ survey four months after the program went into operation pointed out that the Talmadge amendment had created "bitterness and confusion" among the participating welfare and manpower offices, and that

> officials of many welfare agencies simply do not believe in the concept of workfare and do not feel it will work. Some not only predicted failure of the program but indicated that they would attempt to defy implementation of the Talmadge amendment.[29]

While the Talmadge amendment was apparently acceptable enough to Congress, its feasibility as a strong work requirement, in practice, is questionable.

CONCLUSIONS

The unique problems inherent in the incentive approach to encouraging work are centered around the inevitable

conflict between benefits, incentives, and cost. The two
conditions that produce work effort are low tax rates and
low benefits: people need to earn in order to survive if
benefits are low, and they will work more if they can keep
more of what they earn. However, low tax rates increase
both the number of families eligible and the grant to each
family, thus proving too costly. Low benefits are both in-
humane and politically unfeasible.

Benefits also affect the work-welfare choice by being
in competition with wages. When employable recipients are
involved, the principle of "less eligibility" becomes pertinent to the choice between work and welfare. Either wages
need to be raised or benefits lowered if work is the desired
outcome; when benefits are raised, wages need to be raised
accordingly. As Blanche Bernstein said, the question is

> whether in view of the present relationship
> between welfare benefits and wage rates for
> unskilled and semi-skilled jobs, an incentive
> can be offered sufficient to entice welfare
> recipients into employment without disturbing
> the non-welfare population working at the
> same low-paid jobs, and without encouraging
> them to get on welfare.[30]

The use of incentives to promote work effort is new and
represents a change in assistance philosophy. Welfare, before, was seen as an income-maintenance means of "last resort" and the decision to take welfare was viewed as involuntary. It is now acknowledged that many recipients have
some choice of income-retrieval sources, one of which is
work. If society is willing to permit a choice between work
and welfare, it must use incentives to induce recipients to
work. Incentives, therefore, must be high enough to offset
the equally feasible choice of welfare. Incentives in FAP
and H.R.1 failed in this respect. They were gradually weak-
ened to accommodate to the competitive goals of cost and
adequacy and thus ended in being no higher than the incentives in AFDC, which, as was seen in Chapter 4, did not have
the effect of increasing work effort. Furthermore, in order
for disregards to have an effect, they need to be accompa-
nied by an accurate reporting system by recipients and, as
Handler says, "proper, comprehensive supervision by welfare
officials."[31] Even a low tax rate on earned income cannot
compete with a zero tax rate on unreported income.

Just as the incentive approach to inducing work effort
is not workable, so the work requirement strategy is also
not feasible. WIN work requirements were not successful

(as was seen in Chapter 5) in compelling recipients into the
labor force. The Long plan, which contained a very strong
work requirement, could not pass Congress. The Talmadge
amendment, stipulating a much weaker work-test, did pass
Congress, but like WIN, is failing in implementing the
requirement as the welfare agencies will not cooperate.
Strong work requirements are not acceptable to the liberal
sectors in Congress and in the administration and are not
enforced by welfare agencies where they are regarded as punitive to recipients. Handler cites "bureaucracy" as another obstacle: "One of the important reasons why reforma-
tion by deterrence fails is that the welfare bureaucracy is
incapable of regulation; it is inefficient, complex, fragmented, pluralistic, and understaffed," and is given to "a
nonpolicy of nonenforcement."[32]

The effort to constrict the growth of the AFDC caseload
utilized services (in 1962), incentives, and requirements
strategies. In turn, each of these mechanisms failed to accomplish the avowed goal. Welfare reform, which was a combination of all three, was finally abandoned as being too
costly, too inadequate in its guaranteed benefit, too low on
incentives, and too rigorous in its work requirements. The
incentive problem appeared to be insoluble and requirements
were not acceptable.

There are times in the history of assistance when the
group that is being assisted--whether for reasons that are
in the nature of the group itself or in society's need to
constrain its size and cost--is viewed as containing employable recipients, those who are theoretically able to work
and do without assistance. This formulation is threatening
to the viability of the assistance principle itself, as it
elicits the fear that eventually most employable persons
will become part of the assistance group, thus undermining
the economic fabric that supports the ongoing system.

This generally happens when assistance payments become
equal to or more than wages from working. Society can, at
these times, take three kinds of measures to maintain the
sanctity of work and the viability of welfare. It can lower
assistance payments, provide jobs at higher than welfare
wages, or institute and implement strong work requirements.
At this time, both lowering benefits and establishing strong
work requirements are not politically feasible, while creating a sufficient number of jobs with high wages is too ex-
pensive.

The only remaining alternative--if employable recipients cannot be induced or compelled to become self-
maintaining--is to expel them from the assistance program
altogether. H.R.1 and the Long plan, in some measure,

tried to do this by separating out the employables from the unemployable or "deserving" poor. Jule M. Sugarman, Commissioner of Welfare in New York City, at a conference of the Human Resources Administration on December 1, 1973, offered a proposal to "remove all employable persons from the welfare system" and to allocate them to a national program somewhat like unemployment insurance.[33] Barring this kind of drastic measure, similar results can be achieved incrementally within welfare programs as they stand by instituting eligibility requirements strong enough to keep out employables. This seems to be what is happening at present as the current strategy for constraining the caseload.

The trend now appears to be toward state programs with strengthened eligibility requirements and precautions against fraud. California, for example, "reformed" its welfare system in 1970 and reduced its AFDC rolls. The reduction is attributed to a "closing of loopholes and abuses and tighter auditing and checking."[34] New York has gone through a similar experience. In New York City, from 1972 to 1973 the rolls were reduced by 90,000 persons, a drop explained by "increased requirements for documenting need and to management reforms."[35]

This mechanism for caseload reduction is less controversial than federal work requirements and less costly than elaborate work incentives. It is more acceptable to liberals on the theory that the elimination of ineligibles from the program will leave more money and services for the "truly" needy. A congressional study in 1973 points out that 91 percent of all technically eligible female-headed families are on AFDC,[36] so that there is no longer a prevalent fear that the program is not reaching a sufficient number of people. Conservatives are satisfied because "caseloads have begun to level off and should continue to do so."[37]

While the states, in the absence of federal welfare reform, initiated their own programs of eligibility control, the federal government eventually came around to this position, too. In an effort to allow the states more flexibility in pursuing this route, the HEW Social and Rehabilitation Service recently issued regulations to "require welfare applicants to submit a written, signed application" and to "allow instances in which an agency can discontinue or reduce assistance to a recipient without advance notice." The purpose of these and other such regulations, according to Caspar Weinberger, head of HEW, is to improve eligibility procedures "to make sure welfare funds get to those in need. . . . The longer large overpayments and payments to ineligible recipients continue, the more people in real need are deprived of funds intended for them."[38]

The strengthening of eligibility requirements will have the effect of keeping many female-headed families, which had been eligible before, out of the welfare system. Rigorous penalties for not reporting income, for not disclosing the whereabouts of absent fathers, and other such strictures will make the welfare choice less palatable and, finally, less available. So that while the strategies of services, incentives, and requirements had no noticeable effect on the work-welfare choice, the current and coming effort to tighten eligibility will very much constrict that choice, and thereby leave the work option more exigent.

NOTES

1. Social Security Amendments of 1971, U.S. Senate, Committee on Finance, Hearings (Washington, D.C., 1971), pp. 374, 375.

2. Robert F. McNown, "The Story of the Family Assistance Plan," Current History 65, no. 384 (August 1973): 60.

3. The Family Assistance Act of 1970, Summary, U.S. House of Representatives, Committee on Ways and Means (Washington, D.C., 1970), p. 4.

4. Family Assistance Act of 1970, U.S. Senate, Committee on Finance, Hearings (Washington, D.C., 1970), p. 838.

5. Ibid.

6. Joel F. Handler, "Federal-State Interests in Welfare Administration," Issues in Welfare Administration, Studies in Public Welfare, U.S. Congress, Joint Economic Committee (Washington, D.C., 1973), p. 27.

7. Findings of the 1971 AFDC Study, U.S. Department of Health, Education and Welfare (Washington, D.C., 1971), Table 34.

8. Robert F. Smith and W. Joseph Heffernan, "Work Incentives and Welfare Reform: The FAP Experience," Mississippi Valley Journal of Business and Economics 7, no. 1 (Fall 1971): 14.

9. Findings of the 1971 AFDC Study, op. cit.

10. Joel F. Handler, Reforming the Poor (New York: Basic Books, 1972), p. 105.

11. Social Security Amendments of 1971, op. cit., p. 35.

12. Henry J. Aaron, Why Is Welfare So Hard to Reform?, Studies in Social Economics (Washington, D.C.: The Brookings Institution, 1973), p. 53.

13. Sar A. Levitan, Martin Rein, and David Marwick, Work and Welfare Go Together (Baltimore: Johns Hopkins University Press, 1972), p. 123.

14. All the provisions of the Long plan are taken from Social Security and Welfare Reform, Summary of the Principal

Provisions of H.R.1 as Determined by the Committee on Finance, 92d Cong., 2d Sess. (1972).

15. Aaron, op. cit., p. 42.

16. Ibid., p. 43.

17. Child Care Arrangements of AFDC Recipients Under the Work Incentive Program, U.S. Department of Health, Education and Welfare (Washington, D.C., 1972), Table 2.

18. Social Security and Welfare Reform, U.S. Senate, Committee on Finance (Washington, D.C., 1972), p. 77.

19. New York Times, December 15, 1971.

20. Special Analysis, Budget of the U.S. Government, 1973, Office of Management and Budget (Washington, D.C., 1972), p. 185.

21. Manpower Report of the President, U.S. Department of Labor (Washington, D.C., 1973), p. 39.

22. Leonard J. Hausman, "The Politics of a Guaranteed Income: The Nixon Administration and the Family Assistance Plan--A Review Article," Journal of Human Resources 8, no. 4 (Fall 1973): 420.

23. Second Quarterly Status Report, U.S. Department of Labor (Washington, D.C., 1972), p. 1.

24. New York Times, April 20, 1973.

25. Auerbach Associates, An Impact Evaluation of the Work Incentive Program, Vol. I (Philadelphia, 1972), pp. 1-15.

26. David W. Lyon et al., Employment and Job Training Programs for Welfare Recipients in New York City, Human Resources Administration, City of New York (New York, December 1973), pp. 111-13.

27. Ibid., p. x.

28. Work Incentive Program, U.S. Senate, Committee on Finance, Hearings (Washington, D.C., 1972), p. 44.

29. New York Times, October 9, 1972.

30. Blanche Bernstein, "Welfare in New York City," City Almanac 4, no. 5 (February 1970): 8.

31. Handler, Reforming the Poor, op. cit., p. 147.

32. Ibid., p. 145.

33. Jule M. Sugarman, "Welfare Research: A Key to Welfare Reform," Address, Welfare Research Conference, New York City, December 1, 1973, p. 11.

34. Karen E. DeWitt, "Administration Task Force Develops Plans to Overhaul the Welfare System," National Journal Reports 5, no. 36 (September 1973): 1318.

35. New York Times, November 23, 1973.

36. Ibid., November 4, 1973.

37. Ibid.

38. DeWitt, op. cit.

Aaron, Henry J., 109
Abbott, Grace, 3
ADC (Aid to Dependent Children), see AFDC
ADC-UP, see AFDC-UP
AFDC (Aid to Families with Dependent Children): and child care, 8, 9, 14, 59, 64, 76; cost of, 10-11, 12, 101; earnings in, 7-10, 27, 38; and tax rates, 10, 44; and welfare benefits, 6-8, 10-11, 40-43, 49, 102; and work effort, 9, 10, 26-28, 34, 35; and work expenses, 44, 45, 64, 73; and work incentives, 14, 44-50; and working poor, 42; and work requirements, 5, 8-10, 13, 14
AFDC-UP, 13, 84, 85, 87, 89, 94, 95, 116, 117
American Public Welfare Association, 10
Appel, Gary L., 68-70
Auerbach Associates, 88, 91, 92, 94, 96, 115

Barr, N. A., 74, 76
Bell, Winifred, 3, 8
Bernard, Sydney E., 22, 52, 55, 57-58
Bernstein, Blanche, 118
Blackwell, Gordon W., 23, 24, 26
Buell, Bradley, 20
Burgess, Elaine M., 21, 23, 25, 26

Carter, Genevieve W., 22, 45, 75
Case turnover, 22-24

Caseworkers, 46, 48-49, 76, 87-88, 89, 93, 94, 105, 106, 114
Charity Organization Society, 1-3
Child care: and AFDC, 8, 9, 14, 59, 64, 76; and FAP, 103; and H.R.1, 108; and Long Plan, 110; and Mothers' Pensions, 1-4; and Talmadge Amendment, 115; and "Thirty and One-Third," 68; and WIN, 85-87, 88, 89, 96
Cohen, Wilbur, 11
Coll, Blanche D., 4
CWT (Community Work and Training programs), 13-14, 16, 84-85, 93
Cost of program: AFDC, 10-11, 12, 101; FAP, 106-07; H.R.1, 108-10; Long Plan, 113-14; Talmadge Amendment, 117; WIN, 85, 87, 96-97
Cox, Irene, 75
Cultural transmission, 51, 54-56
Culture of poverty, 50, 52, 55

De Schweinetz, Elizabeth, 7
Durbin, Elizabeth F., 41, 45

Earnings: as evaluation of "Thirty and One-Third," 62, 63, 87-90, 93-99, 101, 104-09; disregarded, 49-50; in AFDC, 7-10, 27, 38; in relation to education, 37-38; in relation to welfare benefits, 41-44; in the North, 39-40

Education, 36-40, 66
Employables, 4, 6, 8, 13, 84, 85, 90, 91-92, 93, 97, 106, 108-09, 110-11, 119-20

FAP (Family Assistance Plan), 103-07, 108-10, 111, 112, 115
Family structure, 51, 52-53, 54, 59
Federal Emergency Relief Administration, 4, 5-6
Federal financial participation, 5, 6, 12, 13, 85, 101-02, 108-09, 110, 111, 115
Franklin, David S., 92

Gilbert, Charles E., 11
Goldstein, Jon H., 94-95
Goodman, Leonard H., 28-29, 34, 35, 36, 56
Gordon, David M., 41, 42-43
Gould, Raymond F., 23, 24, 26
Greenleigh Associates, 23, 24, 25, 55
Grigsby, William G., 23, 24

Hall, R. E., 74, 76
Handler, Joel F., 35, 45, 49, 88, 118
Hannerz, Ulf, 52, 55
Hausman, Leonard J., 45, 76, 116
Heffernan, Joseph Jr., 76, 107
Henderson, George, 58
Hollingsworth, Ellen Jane, 35, 45, 49, 88
H.R.1, 107-10, 111, 112, 115, 118, 119
Human Resources Administration, 25

Illegitimacy, 8, 12, 16, 20, 50-51, 54, 101
Income accrual, 22, 28, 56-58
In-kind benefits, 29, 41, 97, 104, 107, 109, 112

Irregular work, 21-22, 25, 26-27, 29, 34, 35, 48-49, 58, 59

Jobs: attaching incentives to, 81; in the Long Plan, 110; in the Talmadge Amendment, 116; in welfare reform, 119; in WIN, 84, 90-92, 96-98; irregular market, 29; to compete with work and welfare, 29
Johnson, William A., 41-42

Kennedy, John F., 12
Kreisberg, Louis, 55
Kronick, Jane C., 52, 55, 56

Labor market, 6, 10, 20, 21, 22, 27, 33, 34, 40, 42, 64, 67, 70, 84, 85, 86, 97, 117
Lansdale, Robert T., 3
Lerman, Robert I., 76-77
Levitan, Sar A., 88, 95, 109
Lewis, Oscar, 50fn, 55
Liebow, Elliot, 52-53
Lifestyle, 30, 33, 34, 49-58
Long Plan, 110-14, 119
Lower-class, 50-53, 54-55
Lurie, Irene, 12

Marwick, David, 88, 95, 109
Miller, S. M., 21
Miller, Walter B., 11, 50
Mothers' Pensions, 1-4
Moynihan, Daniel Patrick, 52

National Analysts study, 67
New York Times, 117

Occupation, 3, 8, 22, 26, 36-38, 50
Opton, Edward M. Jr., 38, 45-46

Piore, Michael J., 48
Podell, Lawrence, 34, 38, 55
Price, Daniel O., 21, 23, 25, 26

Protective payee, 93, 94,
103, 106, 113

Rainwater, Lee, 52-54, 57
Refusal to participate in
manpower programs, 84, 93,
94-96, 103
Reid, William J., 88, 91, 97
Rein, Martin, 21, 59, 88, 95,
109
Ribicoff, Abraham, 12
Roosevelt, Franklin Delano, 4

Sanctions: and FAP, 104,
106; and H.R.1, 108-09; and
Long Plan, 113-14; and Tal-
madge Amendment, 116; and
WIN, 85-86, 93-96, 97-98
Schlenker, Robert E., 68-70,
71
Schottland, Charles I., 9
Schorr, Alvin L., 74, 75
Schwartz, Michael, 58
Smith, Audrey D., 88, 91, 97
Smith, Robert F., 107
Smith, Vernon K., 70, 71, 72
Social Security Board, 6-9
Social services: as a reduc-
tion strategy, 73, 119,
120; child care, 64; con-
gressional disillusionment
with, 85; in H.R.1, 108;
in the 1962 Amendments,
11-13, 14-15; in the Tal-
madge Amendment, 115
Social work professionals,
2, 5, 8, 11, 12, 15-17, 88,
90
Solarz, Andrew K., 45
State supplements, 104, 107,
109, 111, 112
Sugarman, Jule M., 120
Supervision, 2, 3, 4

Talmadge Amendment, 98,
114-17, 119
Tax rates: and AFDC, 10, 44;
and FAP, 103-04, 106-07;

and H.R.1, 109; and Long
Plan, 112; and Talmadge
Amendment, 117; and "Thirty
and One-Third," 65, 73-79

Ulusan, Aydin, 70, 71
Unemployed Parent amendment
(UP), see AFDC-UP
Unemployment, 4, 13, 46, 66-
67, 69, 70, 97
U.S. Children's Bureau, 4-6
U.S. Congress: and FAP,
103-05, 107, 109-10; and
H.R.1, 108; and interest
in employment, 21; and
Long Plan, 110, 119; and
1962 Amendment, 16; and
Social Security Act, 4-6;
and Talmadge Amendment,
114, 116, 117, 119; and
"Thirty and One-Third," 33,
46, 47
U.S. Department of Health,
Education and Welfare (HEW):
discretion of, 108; and
FAP, 103, 105; and H.R.1,
109; Publication (1964),
12, 14, 16; Social and Rehabilitation Service, 120;
Study (1961), 9, 23, 69;
Study (1967), 69; Study
(1969), 42, 69, 95; Study
(1971), 65, 69; and Tal-
madge Amendment, 115, 117;
and WIN, 87, 89, 94, 106
U.S. Department of Labor, 41,
91, 103, 105, 106, 108,
115, 116, 117
Unreported work, 11, 12, 29,
43, 48-49, 58, 59, 74, 76,
118, 120-21

Valentine, Charles A., 22,
29, 55, 56-57
Volunteers (for manpower programs), 87-89, 92, 94-95,
96, 110, 111, 114-16

Weinberger, Caspar W., 120
Welfare benefits: and AFDC,
    6–8, 10–11, 40–43, 49, 102;
    and FAP, 103, 104, 106, 107;
    and H.R.1, 108–10; and Long
    Plan, 111–12; and Mothers'
    Pensions, 2–4; and Talmadge
    Amendment, 117; and
    "Thirty and One-Third,"
    75–79, 80–81
Welfare stigma, 55, 56, 97
Wishnov, Barbara, 20fn
Work effort: and AFDC, 9,
    10, 26–28, 34, 35; and
    disregarded income, 48, 49;
    effect of welfare benefits
    on, 43; and Long Plan, 112,
    113; and Mothers' Pensions,
    3, 4; North-South differ-
    ences, 38–40; relative to
    education, 36–38; and Tal-
    madge Amendment, 117, 118;
    and "Thirty and One-Third,"
    46, 47, 64, 65–75, 76–81;
    and WIN, 90, 92, 96, 97–98
Work expenses: and AFDC, 44,
    45, 64, 73; and CWT, 14;
    and Long Plan, 113; and

"Thirty and One-Third," 70,
    71, 75, 76
Work history, 26–28, 34–35
WIN (Work Incentive program),
    84–98, 101, 104–05, 106,
    114–16, 118
Work incentives: and AFDC,
    14, 44–50; and FAP, 107;
    and H.R.1, 108–10; knowl-
    edge of, 45, 68; and Long
    Plan, 111–14; and Talmadge
    Amendment, 117; and "Thirty
    and One-Third," 21, 29, 33,
    64–81, 101–02; and WIN, 98
Working poor: and AFDC, 42;
    and FAP, 104, 107; and
    H.R.1, 109; and "Thirty and
    One-Third," 46, 47, 64,
    102, 103
Work relief, 4, 5, 21–22
Work requirements: and
    AFDC, 5, 8–10, 13, 14;
    and FAP, 104–06; and H.R.1,
    107–09; and Long Plan, 111,
    113, 114; and Talmadge
    Amendment, 114, 115; and
    WIN, 21, 84–85, 87, 88,
    89, 96–98, 102

MILDRED REIN was, until recently, a Research Associate of the Social Welfare Regional Research Institute at Boston College. She has had extensive experience in the field of welfare, including six years with the New York City Welfare Department (currently the Human Resources Administration). She wrote a prizewinning Masters thesis on "Public Assistance in Barbados," and has had several articles published on this subject in such journals as <u>Social Service Review</u>, <u>Welfare in Review</u>, and <u>Poverty and Human Resources Abstracts</u>. Ms. Rein received her B.A. in philosophy from Brooklyn College and her M.S. in social work from Boston University.